THE LETHBRIDGE-STEWART QUIZ BOOK

Compiled by Mark Jones

CANDY JAR BOOKS • CARDIFF

Editor: Shaun Russell
Cover: Richard Young
Editorial: Lauren Thomas & William Rees

Starwatch cover photograph courtesy of Chris Leach

Published by
Candy Jar Books
Mackintosh House
136 Newport Road, Cardiff, CF24 1DJ
www.candyjarbooks.co.uk

A catalogue record of this book is available
from the British Library

Printed and bound in the UK by
4edge, 22 Eldon Way, Hockley, Essex, SS5 4AD

INTRODUCTION

I was five years old when *Doctor Who* began, back in those black and white days of the early sixties. I was terrified by the Mondas Cybermen from William Hartnell's last story, *The Tenth Planet*, but it wasn't until the later Patrick Troughton stories, and then those of Jon Pertwee, that *Doctor Who* became an integral part of my life.

When Candy Jar Books invited me to compile a quiz book centred around the Brig, I couldn't wait to get started. Here was a character who'd meant a great deal to me as a child, who represented discipline and stoicism in the face of trouble, who met danger with that infamous Lethbridge-Stewart humour. It also gave me an excuse to watch all my favourite Brigadier stories again!

Altogether, Lethbridge-Stewart appeared in twenty-three *Doctor Who* stories. The majority of the Brigadier's stories were from the 'classic' era, with the character first appearing in the Second Doctor (Patrick Troughton) story *The Web of Fear*, facing off against the return of the Yeti (this time at home in the London Underground). He appeared again in *The Invasion*, before being reintroduced at the start of the Third Doctor's reign in the first story of season seven, *Spearhead From Space*, and last appearing in *Battlefield* opposite the Seventh Doctor (Sylvester McCoy).

With the Third Doctor exiled on Earth in 1970, the scene was set for a series of Earth-based adventures, normally involving an alien threat or invasion. Against this backdrop, the series saw the introduction of UNIT, a military presence whose task it was to battle such occurrences, under the command of Brigadier Lethbridge-Stewart. While the Doctor more often than not clashed with UNIT's military mindset, the Brigadier and the Third Doctor formed a strong bond of friendship, alongside other recurring characters including Jo Grant, Captain Yates and Sergeant Benton, who formed the UNIT 'family'.

Such was the popularity of the character, played with aplomb, bombast and a twinkle in the eye by Nicholas Courtney, the Brigadier continued to feature in *Doctor Who* stories and various spin-offs, including *The Sarah Jane Adventures*, The Big Finish audio stories, comic strips and most recently the Candy Jar Books *Lethbridge-Stewart* novel series. As a mark of both respect and recognition, upon Nicholas Courtney's death in 2011, the *Doctor Who* television story *The Wedding of River Song* included a line of dialogue announcing the Brigadier had passed away peacefully in a nursing home. Even so, in a somewhat controversial twist, the Brigadier appeared one last time, as a Cyberman avatar opposite Peter Capaldi's Twelfth Doctor in *Death in Heaven*. Opinion was split on this adventure, some reflecting the character should have been laid to rest following Nicholas Courtney's death, whilst others saw it as a fitting and heroic closure for the character.

This book predominantly features questions about the television series and the Candy Jar Books range of *Lethbridge-Stewart* novels. However, there are also brain-teasers covering the Target novels, the Big Finish audio stories, the BBC novels, the Virgin novels and one or two other surprises. There's something for everyone. This is a book that will provide hours of entertainment and a challenge to the old grey matter. It's a book for dipping into whenever you feel like challenging yourself or your friends – hopefully without too many arguments – or, alternatively, working your way through the questions yourself, chapter by chapter, climbing the military ladder to achieve the rank of Brigadier.

I have to thank my long-suffering wife, who, although not a *Doctor Who* fan, has tolerated my devotion to the show for years. While I monopolised the lounge, working my way through the Brigadier's appearances, she made do with watching her favourite shows on the television in the kitchen without a single complaint. It's been an absolute labour of love working on this book, and I hope it will provide you with as much enjoyment as it did for me compiling it

Mark Jones

PERSONAL CHALLENGES

There are twelve challenges that need to be undertaken to work your way up the ranks. Each test consists of sixty-five random questions. No test is harder or simpler than any other – they are all designed to test your knowledge of Brigadier Lethbridge-Stewart and the *Doctor Who* world(s) he featured in to a greater and lesser degree.

We'll assume that you are already a Private. Consequently, the first Test will be for the rank of Lance Corporal.

Good luck. Fall in for Test 1!

QUESTIONS

TEST 1:

FOR THE RANK OF LANCE CORPORAL

1. What did UNIT first stand for?

2. And what does UNIT stand for now?

3. Name the actor who played Brigadier Lethbridge-Stewart.

4. In the New Adventures novel *The Dying Days* by Lance Parkin, how does the Brigadier say his father died?

5. Who wrote the TV story *The Claws of Axos*?

6. How does the Doctor describe the Intelligence in *The Web of Fear*?

7. What does the Doctor see in his dream in the first episode of *The Time Monster*?

8. *The Daemons* was credited to Guy Leopold. For whom was this a pseudonym?

9. The Master is disguised as a vicar in *The Daemons*. What is he calling himself?

10. Who wrote the television story *Mawdryn Undead*?

11. What has the Master stolen which causes the Time Lords to intervene in *Colony in Space*?

12. In the first episode of *Colony in Space* what does the Brigadier tell the Doctor about the latest field reports?

13. Who wrote *The Invasion*?

14. In *Spearhead From Space* to which location do UNIT track the first meteorites?

15. In *The Mind of Evil* what conference is taking place in London?

16. In the Candy Jar novel *The Dreamer's Lament* when a train travelling from Paddington to Bristol Temple Meads goes missing, into what strange phenomenon does Harold Chorley

believe it has vanished?

17. After the TARDIS lands in a park in the first episode of *Invasion of the Dinosaurs* where does the Doctor tell Sarah he set the co-ordinates for?

18. Who played Dr Quinn in *Doctor Who and the Silurians*?

19. What is the name of the tramp in *The Claws of Axos* and who played him?

20. To whom has Professor Travers sold the Yeti in the first episode of *The Web of Fear*?

21. Name the fashion photographer in *The Invasion*.

22. What do the Doctor and the Brigadier discover when they arrive at Wenley Hospital in *Doctor Who and the Silurians* and what action does the Brigadier take against the hospital consultant?

23. How does the Brigadier describe his situation when talking to Captain Yates over the radio from the Newton Institute in *The Time*

Monster?

24. What honours has the Brigadier received?

25. Which three 'regular' characters made their debuts in *Terror of the Autons*?

26. Where are the radio astronomers based who track Mars Probe 7's lift off from Mars in *The Ambassadors of Death*?

27. Who directed the studio sequences of the final three episodes of *Inferno* when the director, Douglas Camfield, fell ill during production?

28. In which story does the Doctor tell the Brigadier, 'the weapons that you have on Earth are quite nasty enough as it is'?

29. In the Candy Jar novel *The Daughters of Earth* what tune is playing in the pub the Fisherman's Catch when the Brigadier, Anne and Bill ask the locals about UFOs?

30. In which television story does the Doctor say, 'No one's going to turn me into an interplanetary puppet'?

31. In *The Three Doctors* what is the First Doctor said to be stuck in?

32. In the Candy Jar novel *Blood of Atlantis* on which Greek Island do the main events unfold?

33. To whom did the Brigadier give the order 'Chap with wings there. Five rounds rapid'?

34. And who was the chap with wings?

35. Who played Dr Summers in *The Mind of Evil*?

36. In the Candy Jar novel *The Grandfather Infestation* what is the name of the bathysphere Anne Travers travels in?

37. Who played Butler in *Invasion of the Dinosaurs*?

38. Developed by Global Chemicals, what is the refining process to create more fuel from crude oil called in *The Green Death*?

39. In *The Ambassadors of Death* who is in charge of the newly formed Space Security Department?

40. In *The Three Doctors* what tune does the Second Doctor play on his recorder after his 'telepathic conference' with the Third Doctor?

41. Which veteran 'Eastender' actress played Lady Eleanor in *The Time Warrior*?

42. In *Planet of the Spiders* the Doctor tells Sarah that Metebelis 3 is also known as what?

43. How was the television story *Doctor Who and the Silurians* re-titled for the Target Books novelisation?

44. Where does the Fourth Doctor keep the TARDIS key in *Robot*?

45. Who wrote the Tom Baker serial *Terror of the Zygons*?

46. Which actor played the First Doctor in *The Five Doctors*?

47. In the Target Book range *The Companions of Doctor Who* what was the title of the novel penned by Ian Marter?

48. Who played the character of Mawdryn in *Mawdryn Undead*?

49. And in which other 'cult' sci-fi series did he appear as a semi-regular character?

50. To which town does the Brigadier travel in *The Green Death* to collect the cutting equipment?

51. In *The Five Doctors* which villain, of whom Lethbrige-Stewart has been unaware, does the Second Doctor mention when he and the Brigadier are reminiscing about their adventures?

52. In *Planet of the Spiders* what causes the spiders that arrived with the human colonists to grow in size and intelligence?

53. In *The Ghosts of N-Space* during the 1940 London Blitz where does Lethbridge-Stewart spend a night?

54. What is the connection between the *The Sooty Show* and the Doctor Who story *The Daemons*?

55. In the novel *Deadly Reunion* what does

Lethbridge-Stewart enjoy reading?

56. Who played Morgaine in *Battlefield*?

57. In the novel *The Scales of Injustice* who does Lethbridge-Stewart almost shoot on manoeuvres?

58. In which novel does Lethbridge-Stewart speak directly to the UN Security Council about alien threats?

59. What does the farmer remark when he witnesses the TARDIS dematerialise in *The Time Monster*?

60. How does Irongron lose control of his 'Iron Warrior' in *The Time Warrior*?

61. In *Robot* who is Hilda Winters's assistant?

62. In *Day of the Daleks* why can't the Brigadier get a cup of coffee?

63. On the parallel Earth in *Inferno* what does the Brigadier's alter ego wear on his face?

64. In the Candy Jar novel *Times Squared* the

Native Americans who occupied the land where the sentient meteorite fell to Earth call the place 'Manahatuoh', which means what?

65. In *Spearhead From Space* Liz Shaw asks the Doctor what he is a doctor of. What is his reply?

TEST 2:

FOR THE RANK OF CORPORAL

1. In which TV story does the Brigadier's daughter, now the UNIT chief, first appear?

2. And what is her character's name and who is the actress who plays her?

3. What does BOSS stand for in the television story *The Green Death*?

4. Name the two BBC Radio 4 plays set during the Third Doctor's era in which the Brigadier features.

5. What mineral is causing conflict in *Colony in Space*?

6. Which character did Kevin Stoney play in *The Invasion*?

7. To whom does the Brigadier state 'Security. Rather amusing don't you think?' when they first meet, and in which story?

8. Who is the Master posing as in *The Mind of Evil*?

9. In the Candy Jar novel *The Dreamer's Lament*, in their bid for freedom, the slaves of Stedman Manor accidentally contact the Loa using what prayer?

10. What part of the TARDIS is the Doctor trying to reactivate in the first episode of *The Ambassadors of Death*?

11. Who played Professor Stahlman in *Inferno*?

12. Name the character the Master has disguised himself as in *The Time Monster*.

13. In the Candy Jar novel *The Daughters of Earth* for what reason do Sally and Alistair plan to holiday in north west Scotland during February?

14. What 'desolate' coastal UK area was used as a location in *The Claws of Axos*?

15. What suffocates McDermott to death in *Terror of the Autons*?

16. In *The Daemons* who is in charge of the archaeological dig at Devil's End?

17. What is the name of the prisoner being processed during the demonstration of the Keller Machine in *The Mind of Evil*?

18. By what nickname does Turlough refer to his friend Ibbotson in *Mawdryn Undead*?

19. In *Day of the Daleks* what is the name of the British UN delegate who is a key figure at the summit conference?

20. What is the 'alternative community' called in *The Green Death*?

21. In the Candy Jar novel *Blood of Atlantis* the character of Bugayev also appears in a BBC Eighth Doctor novel. What is its title?

22. Who plays Captain Harker in *The Claws of Axos*?

23. In *The Daemons* what does the policeman use

to nail the 'Danger Keep Out' sign to the wooden gate leading to the Devil's Hump?

24. In *Colony in Space* whom does the Doctor say UNIT mistakenly arrested thinking it was the Master?

25. Which actor appeared in both *The Three Doctor* and *The Daemons*?

26. In the television story *The Time Monster* what is TOMTIT?

27. Name the journalist who works for London Television and has been assigned to cover events in *The Web of Fear*.

28. Name the 1981 *Doctor Who* spin-off that starred Elizabeth Sladen as Sarah Jane Smith.

29. In *Terror of the Zygons* what is the Loch Ness Monster revealed to be?

30. What rank is Lethbridge-Stewart in *The Web of Fear*?

31. Name the pressure group wanting to reform Britain along 'rational' lines so that it can be

run by a scientific elite in *Robot*.

32. In which TV story does the Doctor say, 'This is rather like looking for the proverbial needle in the proverbial... just a minute!'?

33. In what vehicle does Lupton escape UNIT HQ in *Planet of the Spiders*?

34. In the Candy Jar novel *The Grandfather Infestation* where does the RAF attack come from?

35. What does Sarah observe about the telephone box when the Doctor can't get through to the Brigadier in *Invasion of the Dinosaurs*?

36. And what is the Doctor's reply?

37. What does the Doctor instruct the Brigadier to do to Wenley Hospital in *Doctor Who and the Silurians*?

38. What business name is first written on the sides of the van used to transport the alien delegates in *The Ambassadors of Death*? The sign then rotates to reveal the name of another business. What is the name?

39. How does the Doctor refer to the Republican Security Forces on the *Inferno* Earth?

40. How does the First Doctor describe his 'replacements' in *The Three Doctors*?

41. In *The Time Warrior* what does the Sontaran describe as 'this hole in space'?

42. The role that the Brigadier plays in *Mawdryn Undead* was originally intended for another character from the Doctor's past. Who?

43. In which comic strip do the Brigadier and the Doctor investigate strange activities at a zoo where naturally placid and docile animals have started to act aggressively?

44. What is the Master's TARDIS disguised as when it lands at the circus in *Terror of the Autons*?

45. Who runs the Buddhist retreat in *Planet of the Spiders*?

46. Who played Chancellor Flavia in *The Five Doctors*?

47. Who played the giant robot in *Robot*?

48. In the BBC Past Doctor novel *The Face of the Enemy* who does the Brigadier enlist to help combat the attack by a fascist version of Earth?

49. In the audio story *The Paradise of Death* what does the Doctor persuade the Brigadier to try out at the Parakon Corporation's theme park?

50. In *The Five Doctors* what is the Fourth Doctor doing when he is abducted?

51. In the BBC Past Doctor novel *Business Unusual* what is the name of the corporation being investigated by the Brigadier and the Sixth Doctor.

52. In the Big Finish audio story *Minuet in Hell* the Brigadier has a hand in which country's devolution?

53. What role did Angela Bruce play in *Battlefield*?

54. In the Virgin New Adventures novel *The Dying Days* the Brigadier collaborates with the

Eighth Doctor during an interplanetary crisis between which protagonists?

55. Where in the hospital do the Zygons imprison the Doctor and Sarah in *Terror of the Zygons*?

56. Who pilots the helicopter flying Lethbridge-Stewart to the site of the nuclear missile convoy in *Battlefield*?

57. In the Big Finish audio story *The Spectre of Lanyon Moor*, whilst Doris is away, what does the Brigadier use so that he can act as an unofficial observer to the strange events taking place on the moor?

58. Who is the Man From The Ministry in *The Time Monster*?

59. How does the Doctor avoid being electrocuted by the electric fence when covertly entering Global Chemicals in *The Green Death*?

60. Name the Trigannon who has been trapped on Earth for centuries in the Big Finish audio story *The Spectre of Lanyon Moor*.

61. Who directed the Third Doctor's first television story *Spearhead From Space*?

62. In *Day of the Daleks* where is it reported that the observation satellites spot troops massing?

63. Which *Blake's 7* actor appears in *Doctor Who and the Silurians* and what character does he play?

64. In the Candy Jar novel *Mind of Stone* what is Prison Officer Fulton's home city?

65. Who played Kate Lethbridge-Stewart in the 1995 direct-to-video spin-off *Downtime*?

TEST 3:

FOR THE RANK OF SERGEANT

1. Who created the character of the Brigadier?

2. What TARDIS component has the Doctor built for himself in the first episode of *Colony in Space*?

3. Name the hospital to which the Doctor is taken in *Spearhead From Space*.

4. Although the Brigadier's daughter officially appeared for the first time on screen in 2012, name the 1995 video spin-off for which the character was originally created.

5. At which London Underground station does the TARDIS land in the first episode of *The Web of Fear*?

6. What does the Master throw into Farrel Senior's car in *Terror of the Autons*?

7. Who directed the TV story *The Mind of Evil*?

8. In the Candy Jar novel *The Dreamer's Lament* what does the Loa reanimate as a grisly message at the dinner table?

9. Who designed the Cybermen as they appeared in *The Invasion*?

10. In *The Mind of Evil* what does the Keller Machine allegedly do?

11. And in reality, what does the Keller Machine actually contain?

12. The actor Geoffrey Palmer plays Masters in *Doctor Who and the Silurians*, but in which popular long running BBC sitcom, with a *Doctor Who* style title, was he a regular?

13. How long does it take the Doctor to solve the mathematical problem that the scientific team in *Inferno* have been working on for a month?

14. How many *Doctor Who* television stories did the Brigadier appear in?

15. What does the Doctor claim to be when discussing the colonists' crop failure in *Colony in Space*?

16. For approximately how many seconds are the Doctor and Liz transported into the future by the TARDIS in *The Ambassadors of Death*?

17. Which country has refused to attend the 'peace summit conference' in *Day of the Daleks*?

18. How is the First Doctor described chronologically by the Time Lord President in *The Three Doctors*?

19. What subject does the Brigadier teach at the public school in *Mawdryn Undead*?

20. To which planet does the Doctor want to take Jo in *The Green Death*?

21. What does Jo tell the Doctor is 'dawning' in the first episode of *The Daemons*?

22. In the Candy Jar novel *The Schizoid Earth* what is the name of the village in East Germany where a large part of the story takes place?

23. What is the name of the Head of the Committee of Enquiry in *The Claws of Axos*?

24. In *The Time Warrior* against whom have the Sontarans been waging war for millennia?

25. How do Captain Yates and Sergeant Benton arrive in Devil's End in *The Daemons*?

26. What designation is given to the vehicle that drives Jamie and Zoe to London when they decide to look for evidence of the Cybermen in the sewers during *The Invasion*?

27. How is the ultimate spider who rules all the others known in *Planet of the Spiders*?

28. Who invented the prototype robot K1 in *Robot*?

29. In the Candy Jar novel *The Grandfather Infestation* what weed killer is used to kill the

Grandfathers and in which TV story does this also feature?

30. What is the name of the shop in which the Doctor searches for transistors, etc in *The Web of Fear*?

31. Who is the leader of the conspiracy in *Invasion of the Dinosaurs*?

32. And what is the title given to the project he is running?

33. In *Terror of the Zygons* what alternative to oil does the Doctor suggest the human race should pursue as a fuel?

34. For *Doctor Who and the Silurians*, at which London station were the scenes of the Silurian plague victims collapsing filmed?

35. In the BBC Past Doctor novel *The Shadow in the Glass* which former colleague of the Brigadier shows him a tape of 'seemingly invisible imps'?

36. What does the Brigadier's alter ego on the

parallel Earth in *Inferno* state the Project Inferno site is?

37. Who wrote *The Three Doctors*?

38. Name the electronics company in Essex that is given red priority security protection by UNIT in *Robot*.

39. Where is the Brigadier teaching when he meets the Tenth Doctor in the comic strip *The Warkeeper's Crown*?

40. In *Battlefield* by what name does Ancelyn call the Doctor?

41. In *The Time Monster* where does Jo say she is ready for a trip to?

42. In which Big Finish audio story does the Brigadier announce the true purpose of UNIT at a press conference, without first telling anyone he would do so?

43. How does the Master refer to the console when he breaks into the Doctor's TARDIS in *The Claws of Axos*?

44. What is the name of the circus owner in *Terror of the Autons* and what does the Master say is his 'real' name?

45. Who directed *Battlefield*?

46. Name the video game in which the Brigadier is one of the characters available to unlock.

47. Who wrote *The Time Warrior*?

48. What is the title of the 50th Big Finish audio story, which included in the cast every single performer of a companion to have previously worked with the company?

49. In *Day of the Daleks* who is in charge of the guerrillas' mission to 20th century Earth?

50. Where do the First Doctor and Susan think they are when they arrive in the Death Zone in *The Five Doctors*?

51. In the Big Finish audio story *Time Heals* why is the UK branch of UNIT under threat?

52. Which actor played the Headmaster in

Mawdryn Undead?

53. In the Big Finish audio story *The Wasting* what is decimating the population of Earth?

54. In what does the Doctor take to the air when chasing Lupton after the latter escapes UNIT HQ in *Planet of the Spiders*?

55. From which television story does this quote come: 'You mean you're deliberately choosing to go on the run from your own people, in a rackety old TARDIS?', to which the Doctor replies, 'Why not? That's how it all started'?

56. In the Big Finish audio story *The Wasting* who does the Brigadier interact with at NATO?

57. In the Candy Jar novel *The Schizoid Earth* what is the name of the ship aboard which the Travers family visit the Arctic?

58. Who is the Director of the Newton Institute in *The Time Monster*?

59. What is the name of the poacher's wife in

60. In the Big Finish audio story *The Blue Tooth* why has the electricity board threatened to cut off the supply to UNIT HQ?

61. When we see Sarah typing her story in *Terror of the Zygons,* what headline has she used?

62. What is the name of Liz Shaw's friend who goes missing in the Big Finish audio story *The Blue Tooth?*

63. In the Big Finish audio story *The Wasting* what is the name of the UNIT Commander who has gone missing?

64. In the Candy Jar novel *Mind of Stone* what was Stanley in jail for?

65. What does Dame Anne Bishop give Lucy Wilson at the end of the Lethbridge-Stewart spin-off adventure novel *The Lucy Willson Mysteries: Avatars of the Intelligence?*

TEST 4:

FOR THE RANK OF SERGEANT

1. What rank is Harry Sullivan when he is seconded to UNIT?

2. What is revealed about the Doctor for the first time when his chest is x-rayed in *Spearhead From Space*?

3. In *The Mind of Evil* in which London street does Benton observe the Chinese delegate in a phone box?

4. In the Candy Jar novel *The Dreamer's Lament* Lethbridge-Stewart surmises that Loa, like the Great Intelligence, may be another version of which inter-dimensional being?

5. In which story does the Doctor say, 'Great Britain always closes on Sundays'?

6. When Masters arrives in London by train in *Doctor Who and the Silurians*, he then hails a taxi to take him where?

7. In the Candy Jar short story *United in Blood* what is the name of Lethbridge-Stewart's old school chum, and what is the name of the pub where he is landlord?

8. Who is the Space Controller in *The Ambassadors of Death*?

9. On the parallel Earth the Doctor travels to in *Inferno*, what positions do Lethbridge-Stewart and Liz Shaw hold?

10. In *The Daemons*, a signpost points to Devil's End (one mile) at the point where the heat barrier crosses the road, but what 'devilish' village is signposted as eight and three quarter miles in the opposite direction?

11. Where is the 'peace summit conference' due to be held in *Day of the Daleks*?

12. In the Candy Jar novel *Blood of Atlantis* what name is given to the silicon-based 'virus' by South African villain Rolph Vorster?

13. Which company is in league with the Cybermen in *The Invasion*?

14. In which Welsh village is the story *The Green Death* set?

15. What are the IMC using to make the colonists think they are being attacked by giant lizards in *Colony in Space*?

16. Where does Jo hide when the Doctor decides to investigate the circus in *Terror of the Autons*?

17. How do the Time Lords reward the Third Doctor at the conclusion of *The Three Doctors*?

18. Where is the atomic research centre based in *Doctor Who and the Silurians*?

19. In the television story *The Time Monster* where was the TOMTIT device built?

20. During *The Green Death* what two disguises do the Doctor adopt?

21. In *The Claws of Axos* what is the name of the American agent from Washington who assists UNIT in their search for the Master?

22. In which television story does Jo Grant first enter the TARDIS?

23. What is the name of the only Sontaran to feature in *The Time Warrior*?

24. How many units of Axonite does Chinn arrange to have transported to the Pentagon and how many to Ottawa in *The Claws of Axos*?

25. What do the spiders in *Planet of the Spiders* insist on being called?

26. Who is the first victim of the Cybermen in the sewers in *The Invasion*?

27. In *Robot* who says 'You mean he's done it again. He's changed.'?

28. Who played the Black Guardian in *Mawdryn Undead*?

29. In *Terror of the Zygons* what does the Brigadier say oil rigs remind him of?

30. In *The Five Doctors* who describes the Death

Zone as 'My shame, and that of every other Time Lord'?

31. In which television story does a newspaper sellers' billboard state: 'Londoners Flee! Menace spreads!'?

32. In which Big Finish audio story does the Brigadier mention his recent falling out with the Doctor over the Silurian incident?

33. In the Big Finish audio story *The Doll of Death* in what 007-related way does Mike Yates refer to Jo?

34. What does the circus owner tell the Master he doesn't need when they meet for the first time in *Terror of the Autons*?

35. What does the Doctor call the Yeti he takes control of in *The Web of Fear*?

36. In the Candy Jar novella *The Life of Evans* what is Evans's first name?

37. Name Irongron's right hand man in *The Time Warrior*.

38. Who steals the blue crystal from Lupton in
    Planet of the Spiders?

39. In *The Sarah Jane Adventures* story *Enemy of the
    Bane* what item does Sarah want the
    Brigadier's help to obtain from UNIT's Black
    Archive?

40. On meeting Sarah in *The Five Doctors* how
    does the Third Doctor describe the Fourth
    Doctor after Sarah's confusion about the
    Doctor's change in appearance?

41. In the Big Finish audio story *Council of War*
    where is Sergeant Benton investigating ghosts
    and missing people?

42. And whilst he is investigating, what is he
    undercover as?

43. In the Big Finish audio story *Vengeance of the
    Stones* where are the two RAF fighter jets
    flying when they disappear?

44. In the same story the Doctor takes a plane and
    retraces the fighter jets' flight plan. What
    happens to his plane and how does the
    Brigadier follow the Doctor's flight?

45. In which television story does the Brigadier state: 'As long as he does the job, he can wear what face he likes'?

46. What does Sarah find on the floor of the apparently mothballed robotics section store room in *Robot*?

47. Which Big Finish audio story in their Short Trips series has the same title as a cult Irwin Allen sci-fi TV series?

48. In this story UNIT are called to Sussex to investigate a railway tunnel. What is happening to the passengers and drivers of trains as they emerge from the tunnel in question?

49. In the first episode of *The Time Monster*, when the Doctor tells the Brigadier he has seen the Master in a dream, what is Lethbridge-Stewart's sarcastic reply?

50. Where does the 'Zygon Harry' hide when being chased by Sarah and the UNIT soldiers in *Terror of the Zygons*?

51. Whilst being chased by the villains in *The*

Ambassadors of Death into what does Liz fall?

52. And with what does the 'Zygon Harry' attack Sarah?

53. Whose car does the Brigadier commandeer in *Battlefield* and what make is it?

54. What is the number plate of the Doctor's yellow roadster, Bessie?

55. In which television story does the Brigadier say this about himself: 'This one goes on until he drops.'?

56. Name the scientist who is a time travel theorist in *Invasion of the Dinosaurs*.

57. Name the poacher in *Spearhead From Space*.

58. In *Day of the Daleks* where is the entrance and exit to the 'time corridor' located?

59. In the Candy Jar novel *The Schizoid Earth* which famous inventor is involved with the creation of the Phoenix?

60. Which television story does this quote come

from: 'Do you not ride the ship of time? Does it not deceive the senses being greater within than without?'?

61. In the Big Finish audio story *The Rings of Ikira* what artefact does the Doctor tell the Brigadier he deciphered?

62. In the Big Finish audio story *The Doll of Death* why is Jo staying in London?

63. On the parallel Earth in *Inferno* what does the Brigadier's alter ego say to the Doctor when the Doctor tells him that 'He doesn't exist in your world.'?

64. In the Candy Jar novel *Mind of Stone* what is the name of the prisoner who befriends Lethbridge-Stewart but then goes to work for Godfrey?

65. How does the Doctor describe the Chronovores in *The Time Monster*?

TEST 5:

FOR THE RANK OF WARRANT OFFICER

1. Who interrupts the meeting between the Brigadier, the Doctor, the head of the committee of enquiry, the American agent and Jo Grant at the beginning of *The Claws of Axos*, and why?

2. Who is revealed to be under the control of The Intelligence in the last episode of *The Web of Fear*?

3. What has been placed in every product manufactured by 'IE' in *The Invasion*?

4. Which famous Welsh character actor plays the hospital porter Mullins in *Spearhead From Space*?

5. In which 'special' TV story does the Brigadier

appear with the Sixth Doctor?

6. During the first episode of *Terror of the Autons* what is the Doctor singing whilst tinkering in his TARDIS?

7. In the Candy Jar novel *The Dreamer's Lament* how does Corporal Dovey meet his untimely end?

8. Where does Captain Yates tell the Brigadier five more looters have been picked up in *Invasion of the Dinosaurs*?

9. In *The Invasion* who is the electronics expert held captive to build a machine that can induce emotions in the Cybermen?

10. Which flower-covered planet does the Doctor offer to take Sarah to in *Invasion of the Dinosaurs*?

11. In *Doctor Who and the Silurians* where does the Brigadier tell Liz Shaw the first overseas victim of the Silurian virus has been reported?

12. Name the story in which the Brigadier meets the Third Doctor for the first time.

13. Which delegate at the London Peace Conference has the Master taken hypnotic control of in *The Mind of Evil*?

14.   In *Doctor Who and the Silurians* what happened to the small planet that was on a collision course with Earth and which caused the Silurians to enter hibernation?

15. What do the project staff in *Inferno* degenerate into when infected by the green slime that bubbles up from the drill shafts?

16. In the Candy Jar novel *The Daughters of Earth*, when Anne Travers first gets their radio working, what does it tune into?

17. Who are the Daleks using as their 'henchmen' in *Day of the Daleks*?

18. Name the 'amorphous blob monsters', apparently expressions of Omega's will, in *The Three Doctors*.

19. Who accompanies the Brigadier to the Newton Institute in *The Time Monster*?

20. What does the Master disguise himself as in

The Mind of Evil and in which other story does he pull the same stunt?

21. What does the Brigadier utter when he discovers the TARDIS has dematerialised in *Colony in Space*?

22. Name the French scientist in *The Ambassadors of Death*.

23. In which television story does a '1929 Humber 1650 Open Tourer' motor car feature?

24. After escaping from the villains' base in *The Ambassadors of Death* Liz Shaw attempts to hitch a ride only to flag down a car driven by whom?

25. What is discovered to be causing the colonists' crops to fail in *Colony in Space*?

26. In the Candy Jar novel *Night of the Intelligence* what is the nickname of Owain's travelling companion Jody Phillips?

27. At the start of *The Green Death* what nearly worn out TARDIS component is the Doctor

working on?

28. In which television story did the Brigadier make his last appearance and who was the Doctor?

29. Who played Irongron in *The Time Warrior*, and what popular ITV adventure series did he go on to become a regular in?

30. In which television story does the Brigadier state: 'Extraordinary muscular control. Very fit that girl. I must adopt some of those movements as exercises for the men.'?

31. What establishment does the robot break into in the first episode of *Robot*?

32. What is the name of the 'strong man' who captures the Doctor at Rossini Brothers International Circus in *Terror of the Autons*?

33. In *The Daemons* what happens when the Brigadier gestures with his swagger stick whilst asking, 'Is that Devil's End over there?'?

34. In the Candy Jar novella *The Life of Evans*

which town is Evans transferred to for retraining?

35. What 'martial art' does the Doctor employ against the Global Chemicals security men in *The Green Death*?

36. Who plays Arak in *Planet of the Spiders*?

37. Name the two difficult and dangerous tasks the robot states it is programmed to undertake in *Robot*.

38. In the Big Finish audio story *The Doll of Death*, it is stated that Jo Grant was what age when she began working for UNIT?

39. How does Bill Filer refer to the nurses whilst he is hospitalised in *The Claws of Axos*?

40. In *The Sarah Jane Adventures* story *Enemy of the Bane* what does the Brigadier use to shoot a Bane operative?

41. In the Big Finish audio story *The Other Woman* (Short Trips series) UNIT are called in to investigate an alien escape pod. Where has it landed?

42. What is Harry Sullivan wearing around his neck when he first appears in *Terror of the Zygons*?

43. In the Big Finish audio story *Council of War* which political party is Margery Phipps a member of?

44. In *Battlefield* Lethbridge-Stewart's UNIT call sign is Greyhound 1. What is Brigadier Bambera's call sign?

45. Who is Sergeant Benton's alter-ego on the parallel Earth in *Inferno*?

46. In *The Five Doctors* how does the Third Doctor describe the Master to Sarah?

47. In the video game *Destiny of the Doctors* the Master is on which planet?

48. What does Nyssa say is missing from the TARDIS in *Mawdryn Undead*?

49. Name the demon summoned by Morgaine in *Battlefield*.

50. In the Target novel *Harry Sullivan's War* how

many years is it since Harry left UNIT?

51. Name the television presenter who introduces the programme covering the opening of the Devil's Hump burial chamber in *The Daemons*.

52. And on what channel is it being broadcast?

53. Which actor played the Sontaran in *The Time Warrior*?

54. How does the Master get Sergeant Benton to leave the laboratory unguarded in *The Time Monster*?

55. In the Big Finish audio story *The Rings of Ikiria* which family owns the farm on which the five 'large circles' appear and where is the farm?

56. What does Liz Shaw pinch from the Brigadier's office in *Spearhead From Space*?

57. In *Mawdryn Undead* at which school is the Brigadier teaching maths?

58. In *Day of the Daleks* what food does the Controller offer Jo Grant some more of?

59. What happens when the army attempt to detonate their explosives in Charring Cross Underground Station in *The Web of Fear*?

60. In the video game *Destiny of the Doctors* what is the name of the champion the Doctors create to challenge the Master.

61. In the Big Finish audio story *The Doll of Death*, whilst on a visit to the National Museum, the Doctor indicates an Egyptian mummy to Jo. What does he reveal about the mummy?

62. In *The Five Doctors* what does the Master describe as 'The black secret at the heart of your Time Lord paradise'?

63. What are the first items the Doctor and Jo discover on Omega's planet' in *The Three Doctors*?

64. In the Candy Jar novel *Mind of Stone* which prison is Lethbridge-Stewart sent to?

65. In which TV sitcom did Nicholas Courtney play the Marquis?

TEST 6:

FOR THE RANK OF SECOND LIEUTENANT

1. Who played the Brigadier's wife, Doris, in the TV story *Battlefield?*

2. What does the journalist in *The Web of Fear* record coming from a telephone receiver to which he remarks, 'Great stuff.'?

3. How does the Brigadier reply when the Doctor forbids him to launch a strike on the heat barrier in *The Daemons*.

4. Where is the mobile UNIT Headquarters based in *The Invasion*?

5. Name the hospital doctor treating the Doctor in *Spearhead From Space*.

6. What is the name of the nuclear missile with a

nerve gas armed warhead which the Master attempts to steal in *The Mind of Evil?*

7. In the Candy Jar novel *The Showstoppers* where do Samson's grandparents originally come from?

8. How many people have been evacuated from London in *Invasion of the Dinosaurs?*

9. In in *The Ambassadors of Death* the computer at Space Control can provide the Doctor with maps of every surveyed planet, but can't provide a map of where?

10. Who is the Executive Director of the Inferno Project in *Inferno?*

11. What tune does the Doctor play on his recorder whilst held captive at Piccadilly Circus Station in *The Web of Fear?*

12. What does the Doctor take from the Master's TARDIS in *Terror of the Autons?*

13. When the Doctor analyses the gun found on the guerrilla from the future in *Day of the*

Daleks, he deduces it was made on Earth, the iron constituent showing it was mined where?

14. What piece of equipment is the Doctor tinkering with in the first episode of *The Time Monster*?

15. In the Candy Jar novel *Blood of Atlantis* what is the name of the Royal Navy ship that Anne Travers boards in order to investigate an outbreak of the silicon-based virus?

16. What 'act' does the 'super species' priest point to on the pictorial history of their planet when Jo and the Doctor are held captive in *Colony in Space*?

17. How did Omega create the Time Lords' power source (for time travel amongst other things) as described in *The Three Doctors*?

18. In which television story does the Doctor first name his home planet of Gallifrey?

19. What is Tegan worried about during the first episode of *Mawdryn Undead*?

20. What do the Silurians use to guard their base in the caves in *Doctor Who and the Silurians*?

21. Name the mind reader the Brigadier and the Doctor go to see at the theatre in *Planet of the Spiders*.

22. In *Robot* what is the name of the Frontiers of Science research centre that Sarah wants to visit?

23. How did the production team on *The Claws of Axos* deal with the unexpected snowfall during location shooting and thus avoid continuity problems?

24. At which iconic London landmark are the Cybermen first seen emerging from the sewers in *The Invasion*?

25. Who supplied the Silurian voices in *Doctor Who and the Silurians*?

26. Who is the local land owner in *Terror of the Zygons*?

27. Outside which building do the Axon monsters attack the UNIT troops in *The Claws of Axos*?

28. In *The Five Doctors* what single-handedly massacres a troop of Cybermen?

29. What is Jo eating for breakfast in the first episode of *The Green Death*?

30. In *Battlefield* the TARDIS lands four kilometres from which body of water?

31. In the Big Finish audio story *The Three Companions* in which country are Jo and her husband, Clifford, based?

32. Who describes the Brigadier as a 'pompous military idiot' and in which television story?

33. Who does the Doctor call a 'ham-fisted bun vendor' and in which story?

34. What does the Doctor tell Liz Shaw the TARDIS has which prevents the Brigadier from getting into it in *Spearhead From Space*?

35. In the Candy Jar novella *The Life of Evans* what's the name of Evans' 'butty'?

36. A diagram of what anatomical feature is chalked on the blackboard in the room of

UNIT's temporary HQ in which the Doctor is working in *Invasion of the Dinosaurs*?

37. Which character begs, 'Spare me the endurance of endless time, the agony of perpetuity!'?

38. Who describes the Doctor as 'A long-shanked rascal with a mighty nose', and in which story?

39. What does Sarah need to collect from the TARDIS to save the Doctor's life on Metebelis 3 in *Planet of the Spiders*?

40. In which television story does the Brigadier see the inside of the TARDIS for the first time?

41. Whose brain pattern does the robot have in *Robot*?

42. The Brigadier was originally not scheduled to appear in *The Sarah Jane Adventures* story *Enemy of the Bane*. Which former companion was the role first written for?

43. In the Big Finish audio story *Council of War*

what does the Doctor build for Benton to help him in his ghost hunt?

44. Name the American delegate to the World Peace Conference in *The Mind of Evil*.

45. In the Candy Jar novel *Beast of Fang Rock* how do Ivan and Owain kill the Rutan?

46. In the Big Finish audio story *The Other Woman* (Short Trips range), what is the name of the alien woman found in the escape pod?

47. What does the Professor believe he will find in the Devil's Hump Burial Chamber in *The Daemons*?

48. What mode of transport and old friend does Lethbridge-Stewart present to the Doctor in *Battlefield*?

49. In the *Virgin Missing Adventure* novel *The Eye of the Giant* what is the name of the millionaire searching for the legendary lost Pacific island?

50. Who wrote the television story *Day of the Daleks*?

51. In *The Five Doctors* what attacks the Second

Doctor and the Brigadier in the caves and
how does the Doctor scare it away?

52. In the Target Books novel *Harry Sullivan's War*
    what has Harry been engaged in developing
    an antidote for?

53. Name the High Priest of Atlantis who is
    summoned by the Master in *The Time
    Monster*?

54. In the Target Books novel *Harry Sullivan's War*
    why was Ian Morter prevented from killing off
    the character at the end of the story?

55. Name the highly volatile liquid used to fuel
    the Doctor's rocket in *The Ambassadors of
    Death*.

56. In the *Virgin Missing Adventure* novel *The Eye of
    the Giant* what is the name of the legendary
    lost island in the Pacific?

57. In the *Virgin Missing Adventure* novel *The Scales
    of Injustice* what does a policewoman start
    drawing unexpectedly?

58. In *Terror of the Zygons* what is located on a bearing of 230/165 from UNIT's temporary base in the pub?

59. To whom and in what television story does the Brigadier say, 'Get off my world'?

60. In the *Virgin Missing Adventure* novel *The Scales of Injustice* 'The Stalker' was created by injecting what breed of dog with ooze from whose drilling operation?

61. In the Big Finish audio story *The Last Post* what conference is the Brigadier preparing for?

62. How do the Doctor and Jo cross the lake of giant maggots in *The Green Death*?

63. In the Candy Jar novel *Mind of Stone* from which port did Lethbridge-Stewart say he would sail for the continent after his escape?

64. Who is controlling the TARDIS when it dematerialises in *Colony in Space*?

65. Who wrote the Candy Jar novel *Moon Blink*?

TEST 7:

FOR THE RANK OF LIEUTENANT

1. Name the white witch in *The Daemons* and the actress who played her.

2. What is hidden behind a secret panel in the offices of 'IE' in *The Invasion*?

3. What are the first words spoken by the Third Doctor when he wakes up in his hospital bed in *Spearhead From Space*?

4. In *The Sarah Jane Adventures* TV story *Enemy of the Bane* what make of car does Brigadier Sir Alistair Gordon Lethbridge-Stewart drive?

5. According to the Doctor in *Terror of the Autons* which alien race invented steady state micro-welding?

6. In *The Mind of Evil* the Keller Machine causes the Doctor to face terrifying mental images of which of his enemies?

7. In the Candy Jar short story *United in Blood* where does Lethbridge-Stewart try to spend a quiet weekend?

8. Who is UNIT's 'technical fellow' as referred to by the Doctor in *The Daemons*?

9. What colour are the roundels in the Master's TARDIS in *Colony in Space*?

10. In the Candy Jar novel *The Showstoppers* what does ex-CIA spook Hanssen wear to stop himself going mad?

11. In *Invasion of the Dinosaurs*, when she is captured for allegedly looting, how old does Sarah say she is?

12. And what is the Doctor's answer to the same question?

13. Who composed and conducted the incidental music for *Doctor Who and the Silurians*?

14. Complete this credit from the end titles of *The Ambassadors of Death*: 'Action by...'

15. Who is the 'top oil rig man' assigned to the Inferno Project in *Inferno* and where was he working when he was summoned?

16. How does Tegan describe the craft on which the TARDIS materialises in *Mawdryn Undead*?

17. In the Candy Jar novel *The Daughters of Earth* what does Judith Edgley give to the Brigadier to shoo him away from where she and the Daughters of Earth are hiding?

18. In *The Invasion* which country has a manned orbital survey space rocket preparing to launch when the Cybermen attack?

19. In *Day of the Daleks* what happens to the captive guerrilla when he is being transported to hospital in an ambulance, accompanied by Sergeant Benton?

20. In the Candy Jar novel *The Forgotten Son* what is the name of Bledoe's local pub?

21. What accident happens when the TOMTIT machine is activated for the first time in *The Time Monster*?

22. Why could actor Frazer Hines (Jamie McCrimmon) not participate in *The Three Doctors*?

23. In *The Three Doctors* the role originally written for Jamie was ultimately conferred on which character instead?

24. In *The Green Death* what is the first victim doing down the pit when he gets infected?

25. What is the name of the Power Complex in *The Claws of Axos*?

26. As the Brigadier informs the Doctor in *The Time Warrior*, who and what has gone missing?

27. Why are the Silurians drawing power from the atomic research centre in *Doctor Who and the Silurians*?

28. Name the poacher's dwelling in *Spearhead*

From Space.

29. From which railway station does Mike Yates collect Sarah in *Planet of the Spiders*?

30. In *Robot* what does Sarah say to the Brigadier to refute him when he says he's a bit old-fashioned?

31. From which TV story does this line come: 'You should be very proud, Doctor. Your knowledge of the past will help to shape the future of this planet.'?

32. In the first episode of *Terror of the Zygons*, when the Doctor arrives, he says, 'I want to know one thing, Brigadier. What is that?' To what is he referring?

33. Who plays the Master in *The Five Doctors*?

34. Who utters these lines and in which story: 'It's a time machine. It was all true then.'?

35. In the Candy Jar novella *The Life of Evans* what is the name of the criminal who kidnaps the aliens?

36. How long does Sarah say the Doctor has been gone after the final events on Metebelis 3 in *Planet of the Spiders*?

37. When the Doctor does eventually return in *Planet of the Spiders* what is his excuse?

38. In *Battlefield* who is the site manager of the Carbury Trust Conservation Area?

39. In the Big Finish audio story *The Three Companions* what is Polly's e-mail address?

40. In the Big Finish audio story *The Other Woman* (*Short Trips* range) who are pursuing the alien woman for her criminal activities?

41. In the Big Finish audio story *The Other Woman* (*Short Trips* range) the alien ship holds statues. Where were they stolen from?

42. In *The Three Doctors* what is the Brigadier observing when he says to the Doctor, 'So this is what you've been doing with UNIT funds and equipment all this time.'?

43. In the Big Finish audio story *Zagreus*, which

two companions meet for the first time and to where do they journey on Gallifrey?

44. In the Candy Jar novel *Beast of Fang Rock* what novel has Bishop just finished reading?

45. Who does the First Doctor team up with in *The Five Doctors*?

46. Who torments the Master when the Keller Machine begins to influence his mind in *The Mind of Evil*?

47. Name the milkman in *The Green Death*.

48. In *Robot* Cabinet Minister Joseph Chambers is killed when the robot breaks into his house and steals from the safe. But what metal was the safe made from?

49. In the *Virgin Missing Adventures* novel *Dancing The Code* to which Arab nation is Jo Grant sent?

50. What type of sandwich does Stuart offer everyone in *The Time Monster*?

51. How does the Master describe his attempts to control the Doctor's TARDIS in The Claws of Axos?

52. In which TV story does the Doctor state: 'Before I was stranded on Earth I spent all my time exploring new worlds and seeking the wonders of the universe.'?

53. Name the short story featuring the Third Doctor and the Brigadier that was published in the 1973 *TV Comic Holiday Annual*.

54. Name the short story published in *Doctor Who Monthly* No. 483, set during the 1968 TV story *The Web of Fear*, which served as a prequel to the Candy Jar *Lethbridge-Stewart* range of novels?

55. What does Tegan mutter when ordered to stay in the TARDIS in *Mawdryn Undead*?

56. How does Lethbridge-Stewart kill the Destroyer in *Battlefield*?

57. In the Big Finish audio story *Council of War* what do UNIT think the ghosts really are?

58. In the television story *Inferno* what gadget manufactured by the Doctor and similar to his sonic screwdriver does Liz use?

59. In the Candy Jar novel *The Forgotten Son* what TV show is John watching in the prologue?

60. How far into the future do the Doctor and Jo travel in *Day of the Daleks*?

61. In the Big Finish audio story *The Last Post*, referencing a TV story, who does the Doctor describe as 'Some damned fool who is trying to drill to the centre of the Earth.'?

62. In *The Time Warrior* which artist does the Doctor tell Sarah he'd like to study under one day?

63. In *Terror of the Autons* why does the Master's dematerialisation circuit not work in the Doctor's TARDIS?

64. How is Dr Lennox killed whilst in the custody of UNIT during *The Ambassadors of Death*?

65. Name four sitcoms to feature Nicholas Courtney in the 1980s.

TEST 8:

FOR THE RANK OF CAPTAIN

1. Name the short film, an extra on the *Mawdryn Undead* DVD, in which Nicholas Courtney reprised the role of the Brigadier for the last time.

2. And what were the Brigadier's final words?

3. What precaution against a nuclear blast does the Master suggest in *The Claws of Axos*?

4. How does Captain Yates give chase when the Brigadier's helicopter is stolen in *The Daemons*?

5. Where is the UK missile base located in *The Invasion*?

6. Who wrote the television story *Spearhead From*

Space?

7. What does Jo say the prison building looks like in episode one of *The Mind of Evil?*

8. In the Candy Jar novel *The Showstoppers* what links The Showstoppers to the cult ITV show *The Prisoner?*

9. By what method does the Doctor make the computer tape disappear and reappear in *The Ambassadors of Death?*

10. In *Day of the Daleks*, what does the Doctor say you can be certain of with politicians?

11. What is the Doctor's reply to the Brigadier in *The Green Death* when the Brigadier states, 'Wouldn't like to have to order you, Doctor'?

12. In the Candy Jar novel *Blood of Atlantis* where is the archaeologist, Sophia Montilla's (aka the Senora) home town?

13. When the Doctor meets the MP in *Invasion of the Dinosaurs* which society does the Doctor state the MP started and what was the title of the book the MP wrote?

14. Who is attempting to penetrate the Earth's crust in the television story *Inferno*?

15. What 'dangerous' plastic flowers are the Autons distributing in *Terror of the Autons*?

16. Who played Sir George Hardiman in *The Claws of Axos*?

17. What does Jo find in the Master's TARDIS in *Colony in Space*?

18. In the first episode of *Inferno* how far has the drill penetrated into the Earth?

19. What do the Doctor and the Brigadier discover behind the hidden door on the spaceship in *Mawdryn Undead*?

20. And what is the Brigadier's droll reply to the Doctor's description of their find?

21. What is the name of the machine the scientists are experimenting with at the atomic research centre in *Doctor Who and the Silurians*?

22. On which planet does the TARDIS land in *Colony in Space*?

23. And in which region of the planet?

24. Who is Head of Security at 'IE' in *The Invasion*?

25. What is the call sign of UNIT HQ and that of the missile escort duty convoy in *The Mind of Evil*?

26. What startles Mike Yates, causing him to knock over a lit candle, when he is surreptitiously watching the Buddhist prayer circle in *Planet of the Spiders*?

27. What is the first thing the Doctor does to demonstrate to Harry Sullivan that he is fully fit in *Robot*?

28. What is the name of the bagpipes-playing pub landlord in *Terror of the Zygons*?

29. Who does the Doctor call a 'blithering Welsh imbecile' in *The Web of Fear*?

30. Who directed *Doctor Who and the Silurians*?
31. Name the location of the radio telescope hijacked by the Master in *Terror of the Autons*.

32. In the Candy Jar novel *Night of the Intelligence* the Vault is technically under the control of what government department?

33. How does Irongron refer to the Sontaran in *The Time Warrior*?

34. Which TV story features this dialogue: 'Frank was telling me his cows have gone dry and my wife's hens have stopped laying.'?

35. In the Candy Jar novella *The Life of Evans* where does Evans turn up naked?

36. Name the Project Leader's assistant in *Inferno*.

37. Who does the Doctor describe as 'galactic ticket inspectors' in *The Time Warrior*?

38. To what rank has Benton been promoted in *Robot*?

39. In *The Five Doctors* which 'phantoms' attempt to confuse the Third Doctor in the Dark Tower?

40. In *The Green Death* who is under cover as the

'man from the ministry' inside Global
Chemicals?

41. In the Big Finish audio story *The Three
    Companions* the Brigadier sends Polly a
    photograph from a UNIT Christmas party.
    Who is Benton dressed as?

42. How long has the spaceship been in orbit
    above Earth in *Mawdryn Undead*?

43. In the Big Finish audio story *Find and Replace*
    what is the name of the alien creature that Jo
    gets stuck in a department store lift with.

44. In *The Ambassadors of Death* the Earth
    astronauts are found by the Doctor on the
    alien spaceship. What do they think they are
    watching on a television set?

45. Where is the Zygons' 'bug' hidden in the pub
    in *Terror of the Zygons*?

46. In *Battlefield* when Ace asks the Doctor how
    he knows the missile convoy is nuclear, what
    is his reply?

47. In the Big Finish audio story *Binary* what is being guarded by UNIT troops?

48. How does the Brigadier refer to the TOMTIT machine when speaking to Dr Ingram in *The Time Monster*?

49. In the Big Finish audio story *Council of War* UNIT has been succeeded by U.G.I.T. What does this stand for?

50. In the Candy Jar novel *Night of the Intelligence* to which city do Anne, Samson and Sally fly?

51. In *Day of the Daleks*, how do the Daleks propose to identify the Doctor when they state his physical appearance does not match their data?

52. In the *Doctor Who* novel *Who Killed Kennedy* what are the names of the journalist and the publication he writes for?

53. In the *Doctor Who Magazine* (issue 467) comic story *John Smith and the Common Men* why does the Brigadier visit the Department of Commonality?

54. How does Anne Travers reply to the journalist's question about what she thinks the Doctor, Jamie and Victoria were doing in the tunnels in *The Web of Fear*?

55. Name the short story featuring the Fourth Doctor, Sarah Jane and the Brigadier that was published in the 1975 *TV Comic Holiday Special*.

56. What does Brigadier Lethbridge-Stewart ask Ancelyn in his last line of dialogue in *Battlefield*?

57. In *The Five Doctors* who is using the Doctors to gain access to the Dark Tower seeking the immortality promised by Rassilon?

58. In the *Doctor Who Magazine* (issue 390) comic story *Death to the Doctor* why have a number of enemies united on board a research base in deep space?

59. What gadget does the Doctor construct out of an empty wine bottle, a couple of corks, two forks and other remnants in *The Time Monster*?

60. And what 'magic' ingredient gets the gadget working?

61. In the Candy Jar spin-off novel *The Lucy Wilson Mysteries: Avatars of the Intelligence* what is the name of the town that Lucy moves to?

62. In the Big Finish audio story *The Last Post* the processing banks of the Apocalypse Clock are salvaged from which 'mad computer'?

63. Who is the General Manager of the plastics factory in *Spearhead From Space*?

64. What confectionery does the Second Doctor offer the Brigadier in *The Three Doctors*?

65. In the Candy Jar novel *Moon Blink* what is the name of Anne's friend and confidant at the vault, who drops her off at the train station when she goes to visit her father?

TEST 9:

FOR THE RANK OF MAJOR

1. What calculation does the Doctor order Jo to answer to prevent her hysterics whilst escaping the Axon ship in *The Claws of Axos*?

2. Which Coronation Street actress played Mary Ashe in *Colony in Space*?

3. How long does Zoe ask for to calculate the trajectory for the missile strike in *The Invasion*?

4. Name the track playing in the background during the plastics factory production line scenes in *Spearhead From Space* and the rock group performing it.

5. Name the prison in *The Mind of Evil*.

6. In the 2014 TV story *Death in Heaven* what

does the Doctor do that Kate Stewart said her father had always wanted?

7. Which famous cold war era comedy film character was originally in line to be the villain of the Candy Jar novel *The Showstoppers*?

8. What does the Doctor condemn the Brigadier with and why in *Doctor Who and the Silurians*?

9. How does the Doctor refer to the white witch when he asks her to untie him from the maypole in *The Daemons*?

10. Which UNIT soldier is killed by the Silurians when they kidnap the Doctor from his laboratory in *Doctor Who and the Silurians*?

11. In which story are the scientists seeking 'a vast new storehouse of energy which has lain dormant since the beginning of time'?

12. In the Candy Jar novel *The Daughters of Earth*, during what historical event does Judith Edgley claim to have been born?

13. How does the Doctor describe his glass of

wine in *Day of the Daleks*?

14. Complete this quote by the Brigadier from *Mawdryn Undead*: 'Take it from me boy, a solid object...'

15. How does the Master trap the Doctor and Jo in his TARDIS in *Colony in Space*?

16. How does the Brigadier normally address Captain Turner in *The Invasion*?

17. When he is captured for allegedly looting in *Invasion of the Dinosaurs*, which side does the Doctor tell the photographer is his best?

18. In what vehicle do the Brigadier and Jo travel to south Wales in *The Green Death*?

19. In the Candy Jar spin-off novel *The Lucy Wilson Mysteries: Avatars of the Intelligence* what is the nationality of Hobo's dad?

20. In the Candy Jar short story *The Dogs of War* who does Lethbridge-Stewart team up with?

21. How does the Doctor describe Bessie's braking system to Jo in *The Time Monster*?

22. Once full of 'human evil' what is the Keller Machine able to do in *The Mind of Evil*?

23. Name the location where the 'cosmic ray research balloon' has landed in *The Three Doctors*?

24. And the name of the Warden who finds it.

25. In *The Ambassadors of Death* how does the Doctor discover their tight-lipped captive was in the military?

26. What 'pretty thing' does Tommy want to show Lupton and Barnes in Planet of the Spiders?

27. In which television story does the Doctor state: 'A new body is like a new house. Takes a little bit of time to settle in.'?

28. What is stencilled on the crates of dynamite that the army are using in *The Web of Fear*?

29. What does Irongron fire at, and miss, with the first of the new weapons supplied by the Sontaran in *The Time Warrior*?

30. How many oil rigs have been destroyed at the start of *Terror of the Zygons*?

31. From which unfinished Fourth Doctor story were clips used in *The Five Doctors*?

32. In *Battlefield* where does the Doctor keep his UNIT passes and whose pass does he give to Ace?

33. Name the man from the Ministry who visits the Doctor's laboratory at UNIT in *Terror of the Autons*.

34. What does Liz Shaw say is odd about the waxwork figures on display at Madame Tussauds in *Spearhead From Space*?

35. In the Candy Jar novel *Times Squared* Professor Travers loses his prized camera while pursuing the Yeti in the Himalayas. Who gave him the camera as a gift?

36. What weapon does the Doctor build to 'capture' a dinosaur in *Invasion of the Dinosaurs*?

37. Where does the Doctor place his hat in *Terror of the Zygons* when he visits Forgill Castle?

38. In the Big Finish audio story *The Three Companions* Polly compares the Second Doctor's hair style to those worn by whom?

39. In the Big Finish audio story *Binary*, instead of calling on the Doctor for help, who does the Brigadier enlist?

40. Why can't the Doctor give Mawdryn and his fellow sufferers the 'energy of a Time Lord' and help them to die?

41. In the Big Finish audio story *The Mega* what machine does Osgood create from the Doctor's blueprints?

42. In the *Virgin Missing Adventures* novel *Blood Heat* what is the Silurian virus known as?

43. Who helps the Doctor regenerate by giving him 'a gentle push' in *Planet of the Spiders*?

44. Name the short story featuring the Third Doctor, the Brigadier and the Master that was

published in the 1973 *Doctor Who Holiday Special*.

45. In *Robot* how is the metal the robot is constructed from described?

46. In the 1991 *Doctor Who Magazine Winter Special* comic story *The Man in the Iron Mask*, where is the Master being held in prison?

47. How does the Doctor describe the trace on the oscilloscope in *The Claws of Axos*?

48. In the 1970 *TV Comic* story *Doctor Who and the Rocks From Venus*, what machine does the Doctor build from some of Bessie's parts?

49. What colour is the TARDIS console in *Inferno*?

50. In the BBC *Past Doctor Adventures* novel *The Devil Goblins From Neptune* it is revealed that the Brigadier can speak which foreign language?

51. What is the name of Global Chemicals' cleaning lady in *The Green Death*?

52. In the *Virgin Missing Adventures* novel *The Eye of the Giant* what is the Brigadier facing an epidemic of?

53. In the Candy Jar novel *Beast of Fang Rock* in what year does Rupert crash land on Earth?

54. In the Big Finish audio story *The Mega*, who told the Mega how to invade the Earth?

55. How does the Master track the UNIT convoy transporting the Doctor's TARDIS in *The Time Monster*?

56. In *The Five Doctors* which phantoms try to trick the Second Doctor in the Dark Tower?

57. Why does the Doctor have difficulty in locating Devil's End in *The Daemons*?

58. In the Big Finish audio story *The Scorchies* what three tasks does Jo need to complete while participating on the Scorchies Show?

59. In *Day of the Daleks* on what vehicle do the Doctor and Jo escape from the Ogrons and guards?

60. What colour smoke do the Doctor's own 'smoking mixture' bombs create in *The Time Warrior*?

61. Who is the Cosmic Ray scientist in *The Three Doctors*?

62. What explosive kills Dr Taltalian in *The Ambassadors of Death*?

63. Who destroys the Intelligence's pyramid structure in *The Web of Fear*?

64. In the Candy Jar novel *Moon Blink* who does Lethbridge-Stewart first notice has been affected by Moon Blink?

65. Where do we learn Liz Shaw has returned to in *Terror of the Autons*?

TEST 10:

FOR THE RANK OF LIEUTENANT COLONEL

1. Name the doctor who treats Turlough and Ibbotson at the scene of their car crash in *Mawdryn Undead*.

2. Whilst the Brigadier sets off to enjoy his regimental dinner in *The Daemons* what does Sergeant Benton say they're stuck with?

3. What do the initials IMC stand for in *Colony in Space*?

4. In *The Invasion* it is revealed that Professor Travers and his daughter, Anne, have gone where?

5. Who demonstrates the Keller Machine in the first episode of *The Mind of Evil*?

6. In the Candy Jar novel *The Showstoppers* what are the names of the TV shows produced by Big Billy Lovac.

7. Who is in charge of the entire military operation in *Invasion of the Dinosaurs*?

8. In which BBC novel does the Brigadier meet the Eighth Doctor?

9. What was the name of the pub in *The Daemons*?

10. In *Colony in Space* who acts as the Master's guide to the primitive city and why?

11. The UNIT convoy transporting the Recovery Probe Capsule in *The Ambassadors of Death* is bombed by what?

12. Why is the Doctor diverting power from the Inferno Project's nuclear reactor in *Inferno*?

13. Who does the American Agent find trapped with him in the Axon spaceship in *The Claws of Axos*?

14. What controls the Autons in *Spearhead from*

Space?

15. In *Day of the Daleks* who makes Jo 'jump' in Auderly House and what does he request?

16. What sign hangs on the door of the lounge in the 'nuthutch' in *The Green Death*?

17. In the Candy Jar novel *The Schizoid Earth*, what is the name of the Russian scientist who helps Travers bridge dimensions towards the end of the story.

18. With the 'fungus stuff' on the move again, to which station does Corporal Lane tell Professor Travers has 'gone'?

19. What does the car that Mike is driving and Sarah is a passenger in almost crash into in *Planet of the Spiders*, only for them to then discover there was nothing in the road?

20. What does the Doctor do to Harry Sullivan in *Robot* when he tries to stop the Doctor taking off in the TARDIS?

21. Who is in charge of the UK missile base in *The Invasion*?

22. Where are the Fifth Doctor, Turlough and Tegan relaxing at the start of *The Five Doctors*?

23. Who does the Master attempt to summon at the end of the first episode of *The Time Monster*?

24. When the Doctor first meets Sarah Jane in *The Time Warrior* what name is she using and what kind of specialist does she claim to be?

25. What is the name of the oilfield in *Terror of the Zygons*?

26. In *Battlefield*, what is Lethbridge-Stewart doing when a call comes through from the Secretary General in Geneva?

27. How far does the Time Lord say he has travelled to deliver his warning about the Master to the Doctor in *Terror of the Autons*?

28. Who is head of security at the atomic research centre in *Doctor Who and the Silurians*?

29. In the Big Finish audio story *The Many Deaths of Jo Grant* what materialises over UNIT HQ?

30. In the Candy Jar novel *The Forgotten Son* what is the name of Ray's debut book?

31. In the Big Finish audio story *The Three Companions* the Third Doctor enjoys a glass of whisky. The whisky was a gift from whom?

32. In which television story would you hear this order: 'All personnel, your attention please. Evacuate Accelerator Section. Shut off all power in your area and proceed to blast wall shelters immediately.'?

33. What does the Master disguise himself as to gain access to the Doctor's lab in *Terror of the Autons*?

34. In the Candy Jar novel *Times Squared*, teasing Lethbridge-Stewart during the flight to New York, Sally Wright compares the cross-Atlantic aeroplane flight to the night bus to where?

35. At the conclusion of *Doctor Who and the Silurians* why is the Doctor studying the Silurians' hibernation apparatus and what does he ultimately plan to achieve by so doing?

36. How does the Doctor temporarily paralyse the giant maggots, allowing Benton to rescue Jo and Professor Jones in *The Green Death*?

37. In the Big Finish audio story *The Scorchies* who is the voice artist for Mr Grizzlefizzle and Professor Baffle?

38. In the *Virgin Missing Adventures* novel *The Eye of the Giant* which member of UNIT sees the interior of the TARDIS for the first time?

39. In the BBC *Past Doctor Adventures* novel *Deep Blue* what is sprinkled on the Doctor's 99 ice cream?

40. In the BBC *Past Doctor Adventures* novel *Verdigris* a spaceship hovers high above London. To the exact size and shape of which railway station is it compared?

41. To what use does the Doctor put his sonic screwdriver outside the enemy bunker in *Robot*?

42. In the BBC *Past Doctor Adventures* novel *Island of Death* name the 'hideous god' the new age

cult worship.

43. Who played the role of Anne Travers in *The Web of Fear*?

44. What is the call sign of the Brigadier's helicopter in *The Mind of Evil*?

45. What makes its first appearance in *Invasion of the Dinosaurs*?

46. What was on the site of Forgill Castle in the eleventh century in *Terror of the Zygons*?

47. Which UNIT soldier does the Brigadier contact via the Second Doctor's walkie-talkie lash up from within the TARDIS in *The Three Doctors*?

48. In the television story *The Time Warrior* what two ingredients are missing from this list: 'Ragwort; Henbane; Love-in-a-Mist; ...'?

49. In the BBC *Past Doctor Adventures* novel *The Devil Goblins From Neptune* where has UNIT US discovered a second Silurian base?

50. How does the Master cause the UNIT convoy to run off the road in *The Time Monster*?

51. And then who do the UNIT soldiers come under attack from?

52. In *The Five Doctors* how does the Brigadier describe his journey to the Dark Tower?

53. In the 1973 *Doctor Who Holiday Special* comic story *Secret of the Tower* where are the Brigadier and the Third Doctor searching for the villain, Hingrad?

54. Whilst in a coma what does the Doctor mutter which leads to a solution to the out of control drill in *Inferno*?

55. And the Drilling Expert says this technique has been used successfully before. Where?

56. In the *Virgin Missing Adventures* novel *Blood Heat* what item does Ace find in the (dead) Third Doctor's pocket?

57. What action does the Brigadier propose on board Mawdryn's spaceship when Turlough says he will lead him to the Doctor?

58. In the *Virgin Missing Adventures* novel *The Scales of Injustice*, by what is the Brigadier distracted, meaning the Doctor decides to investigate matters on his own?

59. On what frequency does the Doctor send out an SOS distress call in *The Ambassadors of Death*?

60. In the Candy Jar novel *Night of the Intelligence* what is the name of General Gore's late wife?

61. What did Oliver Gilbert and Peter Messaline contribute to *Day of the Daleks*?

62. In the Big Finish audio story *Prisoners of the Lake* what is the name of the lake in question.

63. Name the two Target novels based on the television stories that Ian Marter wrote featuring Harry Sullivan.

64. What name does the Doctor give when the Brigadier asks him for his 'real' name in *Spearhead from Space*?

65. In the Candy Jar novel *Moon Blink* how many sets of organs do the Terrae have?

TEST 11:

FOR THE RANK OF COLONEL

1. Who was the driver of the ammunition truck that was hijacked at Holborn in *The Web of Fear*?

2. Now name the Candy Jar Books 2017 publication that continues this character's adventures and the author.

3. What astronomical feature was the result of the testing of the super weapon in *Colony in Space*?

4. Why does the Doctor have difficulty finding his TARDIS at the end of *The Invasion*?

5. Name the *Doctor Who Magazine* comic strip story in which the Brigadier meets the Tenth

Doctor.

6. What is revealed to be on the Doctor's right forearm in *Spearhead from Space*?

7. In *The Invasion* what graffiti is chalked on the wall of the lift shaft when the Doctor and Jamie make their escape?

8. In *The Mind of Evil* it is stated that the Keller Machine has been used successfully in another country. Where and to process how many cases?

9. What misapprehension caused viewers to write to the Radio Times after transmission of the last episode of *The Daemons*?

10. Name the prisoner who assists the Master in *The Mind of Evil*.

11. In the Candy Jar novel *The Grandfather Infestation* which pop singer is the inspiration for Marty Wilde's radio show?

12. What method does the Doctor say is being used to transport the dinosaurs through time

in *Invasion of the Dinosaurs*?

13. What does the Doctor discover when he examines the log book at the atomic research centre in *Doctor Who and the Silurians*?

14. When the Doctor asks after Sergeant Benton in *Mawdryn Undead* what is the Brigadier's reply?

15. Name the TV journalist 'resident' in Space Control in *The Ambassadors of Death*.

16. In what year did the colonists set out from Earth in *Colony in Space*?

17. How does the Doctor regain control of the lorry transporting the Recovery Probe Capsule after it has been hijacked in *The Ambassadors of Death*?

18. Which part of the drill is oozing the green slime in *Inferno*?

19. Who does the Brigadier instruct to blow up the base in *Doctor Who and the Silurians*?

20. In *Day of the Daleks* Captain Yates tells Jo, 'r.h.i.p.'. What does he mean? And in which 2017 television story do we hear this statement again?

21. From where do the miners tell Jo she could seek authority to go down the mine in *The Green Death*?

22. In the Candy Jar short story ' '48 Crash' what is the name of the Radio One DJ?

23. How does Sergeant Benton enter the Doctor's laboratory in *The Three Doctors*?

24. Why does Sarah Jane enter the TARDIS for the first time in *The Time Warrior*?

25. With which professor did Jo Grant travel up the Amazon and later marry?

26. Who are the Master's scientific colleagues in *The Time Monster*?

27. What personal item of the Brigadier's is the mind reader holding when he says, 'You received it in a hotel. A hotel by the sea.

Brighton, was it? From a young lady called Doris.'?

28. What iconic item of clothing appears for the first time in *Robot*?

29. In *The Claws of Axos* what is Chinn seen eating after the Brigadier asks him where he's been hiding?

30. What activates the plastic doll whilst Jo is on the telephone in the Doctor's lab in *Terror of the Autons*?

31. Name the nurse who tends Harry Sullivan after he has been shot in *Terror of the Zygons*.

32. When the First Doctor is abducted in *The Five Doctors*, how does the Fifth Doctor describe the pain he experiences?

33. In *Battlefield* what is the name of the hotel the Doctor and Ace book into?

34. In the Candy Jar novel *Times Squared* Jemba-Wa dubs the tall white-furred Yeti who serves him 'Kabadom'. This means what in Tibetan?

35. Where is the lift located that provides access to the nuclear bunker beneath London in *Invasion of the Dinosaurs*?

36. In *The Five Doctors* how does the Fifth Doctor gain access to the Time Scoop control room on Gallifrey?

37. In the Big Finish audio story *The Three Companions*, due to the flooding of London, where has the British Government relocated?

38. In the *Virgin Missing Adventures* novel *Blood Heat* what does the Brigadier inject into Jo Grant to get information from her?

39. And in the same story what happens to Jo after she receives this injection?

40. What armoured vehicle does UNIT attempt to use to destroy the robot in *Robot*?

41. In the BBC *Past Doctor Adventures* novel *Last of the Gadarene*, what is the name of the East Anglian village that the Brigadier sends the Doctor and Jo to investigate.

42. In the BBC *Past Doctor Adventures* novel *Heart of TARDIS*, what 'quest' does the Fourth Doctor abandon the moment he thinks the Brigadier is in danger?

43. What classic Doctor Who line is quoted by the Fifth Doctor in *Mawdryn Undead*?

44. In the short story *Listening Watch*, published in the 1991 *Doctor Who Magazine Winter Special*, who are UNIT battling once again?

45. Which of the Doctor's hearts does he discover to be beating slightly faster when he awakens from his coma in *Inferno*?

46. After Captain Yates has been hypnotised by BOSS in *The Green Death* what does the Doctor use to bring him out of the hypnotic spell?

47. What happens to the Brig during this process?

48. In the BBC *Past Doctor Adventures* novel *The King of Terror* the Brigadier meets his American counterpart. By what title is this person known?

49. Which famous rugby commentator can be heard whilst Benton and Yates are watching the match from Twickenham in *The Daemons*?

50. In the BBC *Past Doctor Adventures* novel *Verdigris* who is Iris Wildthyme's companion?

51. In the BBC *Past Doctor Adventures* novel *Island of Death* what is revealed about most of the men under the Brigadier's command at UNIT?

52. In *The Three Doctors* the Brigadier asks, 'Who in the name of heaven was that?' Who is he referring to?

53. In the Big Finish audio story *Prisoners of the Lake* what are the names of the three characters that dive down to the lake bed.

54. How is the TARDIS rescued after the UNIT convoy is attacked by a V1 'Doodlebug' rocket in *The Time Monster*?

55. In the Big Finish audio story *The Many Deaths of Jo Grant* what has Rowe created?

56. Name the RAF base where the special plane carrying the delegates to the 'peace summit

conference' is due to land in *Day of the Daleks*.

57. In the Big Finish story *The Scorchies* who do the Doctor and Jo go ballroom dancing with?

58. How is Axonite described in *The Claws of Axos*?

59. What does the Brigadier say when the Doctor begins to regenerate in *Planet of the Spiders*?

60. Where is the entrance to the Zygons' ship located in Forgill Castle in *Terror of the Zygons*?

61. What does the Doctor want to go and choose at the end of *Spearhead from Space*?

62. In the Candy Jar novel *Moon Blink* what is the name of Rupert Slant's new identity?

63. What is the Time Lord dressed as when he meets the Doctor at the top of the radio telescope in *Terror of the Autons*?

64. Who produced *The Web of Fear*?

65. What do the Doctor and Sarah disguise themselves as to gain access to Irongron's castle in *The Time Warrior*?

TEST 12:

FOR THE RANK OF BRIGADIER

1. What is the name of the Devil's End village constable in *The Daemons*?

2. In *Spearhead from Space* the Doctor names a planet where the inhabitants communicate with their eyebrows. Name this planet.

3. Who does the Brigadier put in charge of the escort detail to guard the missile in *The Mind of Evil*?

4. In the Candy Jar novel *The Grandfather Infestation* which Scottish island is infested by the plants?

5. Who is the radio operator of the temporary UNIT HQ in *Invasion of the Dinosaurs*?

6. What does the Doctor pour into Bessie's radiator when it breaks down in *Doctor Who and the Silurians*?

7. What two questions does the Doctor attempt to ask astronaut Van Lyden to ascertain if he is on board the Recovery Probe Capsule when it is returned to Space Control in *The Ambassadors of Death*?

8. When the Doctor arrives on the parallel Earth in *Inferno* what slogan is on the poster he sees on the wall of his workshop?

9. In *Day of the Daleks* what does the Doctor tell Jo he said to Napoleon?

10. Which official does the Master impersonate in *Colony in Space*?

11. What does the Third Doctor find on the TARDIS console just before the Second Doctor appears in *The Three Doctors*?

12. Who is the Brigadier immediately answerable to in *The Invasion*?

13. Name the miner who Jo goes down the pit with in *The Green Death*, and the miner they are going to rescue.

14. In *The Time Warrior* how many hatchings of cadets are there in the Sontaran Military Academy at each muster parade?

15. In *Robot* what clue does the Doctor discover – something that was crushed by a weight of a quarter of a ton?

16. In which novel is the Brigadier's first wife, Fiona, first named?

17. Who composed the haunting incidental music for *Terror of the Zygons*?

18. What animal do the Axons use to demonstrate the properties of Axonite in *The Claws of Axos*?

19. What does the white witch say she and Sergeant Benton must do to celebrate the May Day miracle in *The Daemons*?

20. What local brew is sold in the hotel in *Battlefield*?

21. When the Brigadier begins to overcome his 'amnesia' in *Mawdryn Undead* what is the first monster he sees in his memory?

22. In *The Five Doctors* who is the Brigadier's replacement at UNIT?

23. In his retirement and whilst in his last days in the nursing home, what does the Brigadier always ask the nurses to pour out and why?

24. In the Big Finish audio story *The Scorchies* which Gerry Anderson series does Jo refer to?

25. Who directed the television story *The Web of Fear*?

26. In the Candy Jar novel *The Schizoid Earth* what can you make out of NICKY C and JEZZA B?

27. In the Big Finish audio story *The Spectre of Lanyon Moor* name the pub in which the Brigadier stays.

28. Name the space shot that Earth has lost contact with at the start of the television story *The Ambassadors of Death*.

29. Who composed the incidental music for *The Invasion*?

30. In the Big Finish audio story *The Many Deaths of Jo Grant* the Doctor mentions the TARDIS's fast return switch. In which television story do we first learn of this?

31. What is the call sign of the air strike the Brigadier orders on the Autons coach in *Terror of the Autons*?

32. Who is exposed as a UNIT 'traitor' in *Invasion of the Dinosaurs*?

33. When the mind reader holds the Doctor's sonic screwdriver in *Planet of the Spiders* what monsters does he see?

34. How does Jo describe Bill Filer's look when the American agent has been asked to hand over his prisoner, the Master, in *The Claws of Axos*?

35. In the Candy Jar novel *Times Squared* what song is playing loudly as Lethbridge-Stewart and the response team head into the subway system to corner the Yeti?

36. Name the medical doctor at the atomic research centre in *Doctor Who and the Silurians*.

37. In the Big Finish audio story *Prisoners of the Lake* how does Jo describe what travelling with the Doctor is like?

38. In the *Virgin Missing Adventures* novel *The Scales of Injustice* what were the names of the two guinea pigs given to Liz by her friend in Cambridge when she moved to London?

39. In the BBC *Past Doctor Adventures* novel *Deep Blue* where does a lighthouse keeper report seeing a ball of light plunging into the sea?

40. In the short story *Fond Memories*, published in the 1992 *Doctor Who Magazine Holiday Special*, where do the Brigadier and Sarah Jane meet to talk about old times?

41. And in the same story, John Benton appears on the bill for the evening's entertainment, but as what?

42. Name the television reporter who presents live from the location of the summit conference in *Day of the Daleks*.

43. In *Terror of the Zygons* over which county do UNIT lose track of the Zygon ship?

44. In the BBC novel *Harvest of Time* the Brigadier is starting to 'forget' about UNIT's highest profile prisoner. Who?

45. Who directed the TV story *Mawdryn Undead*?

46. In the BBC *Past Doctor Adventures* novel *The Algebra of Ice*, the Brigadier finds himself helping the Seventh Doctor and Ace investigate what in the Kent countryside?

47. In the short story *A Romantic Evening*, published in *Doctor Who Magazine* (issue 187), Alistair and Doris Lethbridge-Stewart are looking through their wedding photographs. Who suddenly begins to appear in some of them?

48. How does the Brigadier gain access to the prison in *The Mind of Evil*?

49. In the BBC *Past Doctor Adventures* novel *The King of Terror* who are the parents of Johnny Chess?

50. Who directed *Planet of the Spiders*?

51. In the BBC *Past Doctor Adventures* novel *Heart of TARDIS* in what position does the Second Doctor play his recorder?

52. In the BBC *Past Doctor Adventures* novel *The Last of the Gaderene*, what is the name of the former Spitfire pilot who contacts the Brigadier to voice his concerns about strange goings on in his village.

53. Who wrote the TV story *The Time Monster*?

54. In the BBC *Past Doctor Adventure* novel *The Devil Goblins From Neptune* Mike Yates's full name is revealed. What is it?

55. Who shoots the Sontaran at the conclusion of *The Time Warrior*, causing the Sontaran's ship to explode?

56. Where does the Doctor find Gooch, the missing radio telescope scientist, in *Terror of the Autons*?

57. In the 1973 *Doctor Who Holiday Special* comic

story *Fogbound*, where is the beach that is suddenly engulfed in an unnaturally dense fog?

58. In the *Doctor Who Magazine* (issue 234) comic story *Target Practice* who is the Third Doctor approached to work for rather than UNIT?

59. How is the Master's TARDIS disguised in *The Time Warrior*?

60. Name the short story featuring the Doctor, Sarah Jane and the Brigadier that was published in the 1974 TV Comic Holiday Annual.

61. Why does the Doctor suspect all is not as it seems with Major General Scobie's 'waxwork' in Madame Tussauds in *Spearhead from Space*?

62. In the Target novel *Harry Sullivan's War* to where does Harry get posted to work on weapons research?

63. At the conclusion of *The Three Doctors* what does the Brigadier tell Benton they need to do

at UNIT HQ?

64. In the *Virgin Missing Adventures* novel *Dancing the Code* what does the machine the Doctor builds predict?

65. Where is the villain's base located in *The Ambassadors of Death*?

ANSWERS

TEST 1

1. United Nations Intelligence Taskforce.
2. UNified Intelligence Taskforce.
3. Nicholas Courtney.
4. Fighting alongside Field-Marshal Montgomery in Africa during World War II.
5. Bob Baker and Dave Martin.
6. A formless, shapeless thing, floating about in space like a cloud of mist only with a mind and will.
7. A quartz crystal shaped like a trident.
8. Robert Sloman and Barry Letts.
9. Magister (the Latin word for master).
10. Peter Grimwade.
11. Secret information on a device called the Doomsday Weapon.
12. That there's no sign of the Master.
13. Derrick Sherwin (from a story by Kit Pedler).
14. Sector 5, Epping.
15. The World Peace Conference.

16. The Keynsham Triangle.
17. UNIT HQ.
18. Fulton Mackay.
19. Pigbin Josh. Derek Ware.
20. Julius Silverstein.
21. Isobel Watkins.
22. The first victim of the Silurians's plague virus. The Brigadier draws his gun on him to prevent him from examining the dead body.
23. 'I feel as naked as a babe in its bath.'
24. DSO, CMG, CBE.
25. Jo Grant, Captain Mike Yates, The Master.
26. Cambridge.
27. Barry Letts.
28. *Terror of the Autons*.
29. 'I Want You Back' – the Jackson Five.
30. *Day of the Daleks*.
31. A Time Eddy.
32. Santorini.
33. Jenkins.
34. Bok (The Daemons).
35. Michael Sheard.
36. Tethys.
37. Martin Jarvis.
38. The Stevens Process.
39. General Carrington.
40. 'Twinkle, Twinkle Little Star'.
41. June Brown (Dot Cotton in Eastenders).
42. The Blue Planet.

43. *Doctor Who and the Cave Monsters*.
44. In his shoe.
45. Robert Banks Stewart.
46. Richard Hurndall.
47. *Harry Sullivan's War*.
48. David Collings.
49. Sapphire & Steel, as Silver.
50. Newport.
51. The Terrible Zodin.
52. The blue crystals.
53. A public shelter in Eaton Square.
54. Matthew Corbett, son of Harry Corbett, played one of the Devil's End villagers.
55. Science-fiction magazines.
56. Jean Marsh.
57. Marmaduke Harrington-Smythe, the Training Marshal.
58. 'Who Killed Kennedy' (David Bishop).
59. 'Londoners!'
60. The Doctor damages the Iron Warrior's control box by shooting a crossbow bolt into it.
61. Arnold Jellicoe.
62. The canteen is closed.
63. An eye patch.
64. 'The Island Where There is Wood for Bows.'
65. 'Practically everything, my dear.'

TEST 2

1. *The Power of Three* (2012).
2. Kate Stewart. Jemma Redgrave.
3. Bimorphic Organisational Systems Supervisor.
4. *Paradise of Death* (1993), *The Ghosts of N-Space* (1996).
5. Duralinium.
6. Tobias Vaughn.
7. Dr Elizabeth Shaw. *Spearhead From Space.*
8. Professor Emil Keller.
9. La Complainte Du Reveur (The Dreamer's Lament).
10. The Time Vector Generator.
11. Olaf Pooley.
12. Professor Thascales.
13. The Brigadier's birthday.
14. Dungeness, Kent.
15. A plastic armchair.
16. Professor Horner.
17. Barnham.

18. Hippo.
19. Sir Reginald Styles.
20. The Wholeweal Community.
21. 'Emotional Chemistry'.
22. Tim Piggott-Smith.
23. A piece of rock.
24. The Spanish Ambassador.
25. Stephen Thorne: Omega (*The Three Doctors*); Azal (*The Daemons*).
26. Transmission Of Matter Through Interstitial Time.
27. Harold Chorley.
28. K9 and Company.
29. A Zygon cyborg called a Skarasen.
30. Colonel.
31. The Scientific Reform Society.
32. *The Invasion*.
33. The Whomobile.
34. RAF Buchan.
35. 'Probably been vandalised'.
36. 'That's a very unfair word you know, because actually the Vandals were quite decent chaps!'
37. Quarrantine the site.
38. Hay Hoe Launderers Ltd.
39. 'Oafs in uniform.'
40. As a Dandy and a Clown.
41. The Earth.
42. Ian Chesterton. (The actor, William Russell, was unavailable.)

43. *The Arkwood Experiments*. (John Canning: TV Comic Issues 944-949.)
44. A horsebox lorry.
45. Cho-Je.
46. Dinah Sheridan.
47. Michael Kilgarriff.
48. Ian and Barbara Chesterton. The Master.
49. The Experienced Reality Grid.
50. Punting on the River Cam in Cambridge.
51. SenéNet.
52. Malebolgia.
53. Brigadier Winifred Bambera.
54. The United Kingdom and Mars.
55. The Decompression Chamber.
56. Flight Lieutenant Lavel.
57. An 'official' holiday.
58. Dr Cook.
59. He uses a Hy-Mac hoist mounted on the rear of a South Wales Electricity Land Rover.
60. Sancreda.
61. Derek Martinus.
62. Along the Russian Chinese frontier.
63. Paul Darrow (Avon in Blake's 7). Captain Hawkins.
64. Liverpool.
65. Beverley Cressman.

TEST 3

1. Mervyn Haisman and Henry Lincoln.
2. A brand new dematerialisation circuit.
3. Ashbridge Cottage Hospital.
4. *Downtime*.
5. Covent Garden.
6. A 'troll' doll.
7. Timothy Combe.
8. A reanimated steak.
9. Bobi Bartlett.
10. Drain evil impulses from the human mind.
11. An alien parasite that feeds on evil.
12. *As Time Goes By* (BBC 1992-2002).
13. 10 minutes.
14. 23.
15. An expert in agriculture.
16. 15.
17. China.
18. As the 'earliest version' of the Doctor.
19. Maths.

20. Metebelis 3.
21. The Age of Aquarius.
22. Deepdene.
23. Mr Horatio Chinn.
24. The Rutans.
25. The Brigadier's helicopter.
26. UNIT Transport Car 23.
27. The Great One.
28. Professor Kettlewell.
29. DN6. 'Planet of Giants'.
30. M. Thomson Electricians.
31. Sir Charles Grove, MP.
32. Operation Golden Age.
33. The 'energising of hydrogen'.
34. Marylebone.
35. Captain Palmer.
36. A scientific labour camp.
37. Bob Baker and Dave Martin.
38. Emmett's Electronics Ltd.
39. Sandhurst Military School.
40. Merlin.
41. Atlantis
42. *The Coup*.
43. 'What a botch up!'
44. Luigi Rossini. Hugh Russell.
45. Michael Kerrigan.
46. *Legacy*.
47. Robert Holmes.
48. *Zagreus*.

49. Anat.
50. Skaro.
51. The UK Government wants its own military investigative organisation under its sole control.
52. Angus Mackay.
53. A deadly flu-like infection.
54. An auto-gyro.
55. *The Five Doctors*.
56. Commodore Sullivan (a nod to Harry Sullivan).
57. The Amundsen.
58. Dr Percival.
59. Meg.
60. The Doctor is using large amounts of power for his experiments on the TARDIS.
61. 'Another Bermuda Triangle?'
62. Jean.
63. Colonel Brimmicombe-Wood.
64. Burglary.
65. A time ring.

TEST 4

1. Royal Navy Lieutenant.
2. He has two hearts.
3. Cornwall Gardens, SW7.
4. Sunyata.
5. *Invasion of the Dinosaurs*.
6. The Ministry of Science.
7. Bill Cunningham. The Greyhound Inn.
8. Ralph Cornish.
9. Brigade Leader Lethbridge-Stewart. Section Leader Elizabeth Shaw.
10. Satanhall.
11. Auderly House.
12. Mutalith.
13. International Electromatics.
14. Llanfairfach.
15. A survey robot armed with fake claws and a holographic projector.
16. Under a blanket on the back seat of Bessie.
17. By giving him a new, working

dematerialisation circuit for his TARDIS and returning his knowledge of time travel law.

18. Wenley Moor.
19. The Newton Institute in Wootton.
20. A Welsh milkman. A cleaning lady.
21. Bill Filer.
22. *Colony in Space*.
23. Linx.
24. 5 units to the Pentagon, 1 to Ottawa.
25. 'Eight-legs.'
26. A policeman.
27. Sergeant Benton.
28. Valentine Dyall.
29. 'Three-legged spiders in Wellington boots.'
30. The Second Doctor.
31. *The Web of Fear*.
32. 'Old Soldiers.'
33. As Jemima Bond, *License to Spill*.
34. Conjurors.
35. Fred.
36. Gwynfor.
37. Bloodaxe.
38. Tommy.
39. The Tunguska Scroll.
40. All teeth and curls.
41. Kettering.
42. A local councillor.
43. Over North East Scotland.
44. The Doctor's plane crashes into the sea. The

Brigadier follows the Doctor by helicopter.
45. *The Three Doctors*.
46. A pool of oil, on which she slips.
47. *Time Tunnel*.
48. The driver and all passengers are dead.
49. 'Really Doctor, you'll be consulting the entrails of a sheep next.'
50. In the hayloft of a barn.
51. On the canal towpath, beneath the bridge.
52. With a pitchfork.
53. Shou Yuing's. Citroen 2CV.
54. WHO 1.
55. *Mawdryn Undead*.
56. Professor Whitaker.
57. Sam Seeley.
58. A river weir.
59. Nikola Tesla.
60. *Battlefield*.
61. The Rosetta Stone.
62. She is attending a climate conference.
63. 'Then you won't feel the bullets when we shoot you!'
64. Nolan.
65. As 'time eaters'.

TEST 5

1. Captain Yates. To report an in-coming UFO.
2. Staff Sergeant Arnold.
3. A micro-monolithic circuit.
4. Talfryn Thomas.
5. *Dimensions In Time* (30th anniversary Children in Need Special, 1993).
6. 'I don't want to set the world on fire.'
7. He is killed by a reanimated cow.
8. Hyde Park.
9. Professor Watkins.
10. Florana.
11. Paris.
12. *Spearhead from Space*.
13. Captain Chin Lee.
14. It became the moon.
15. Primords.
16. Judith Edgley, the leader of the Daughters of Earth, at the inaugural Women's Liberation Conference in Manchester.

17. The Ogrons.
18. Gell Guards.
19. Sergeant Benton.
20. A telephone engineer. *Terror of the Autons*.
21. 'Doctor. Come back at once.'
22. Bruno Taltalian.
23. *Mawdryn Undead*.
24. Dr Taltalian.
25. Radiation from the superweapon.
26. Jipps.
27. The space time co-ordinate programmer.
28. *Battlefield*. Sylvester McCoy (the Seventh Doctor).
29. David Daker. Boon (he played Harry).
30. *Planet of the Spiders*.
31. Ministry of Defence Weapons Research Centre.
32. Tony.
33. The end of his swagger stick catches fire as it makes contact with the heat barrier.
34. Imber.
35. Venusian Akido.
36. Gareth Hunt.
37. Mining operations. Operations involving radioactive material.
38. 18.
39. 'Florence Nightingales.'
40. A gun hidden in his walking cane.
41. The Kent countryside.

42. The Doctor's long scarf.
43. The Harmony Party.
44. Seabird.
45. Platoon Under Officer Benton.
46. As his best enemy.
47. Siralos.
48. The Zero Room.
49. The Destroyer.
50. 10.
51. Alastair Fergus.
52. BBC 3.
53. Kevin Lindsay.
54. The Master impersonates the Brigadier's voice during a phone call to Benton, telling him he's needed at the house.
55. The Oliver family. Sark, the Channel Islands.
56. The key to the TARDIS.
57. Brendon Public School.
58. Grapes.
59. They fail to explode as they have been covered in the Yeti's 'web material'.
60. The Graak.
61. That he knew the person in question in real life.
62. The Death Zone.
63. The water cooler and the Brigadier's computer.
64. Wormwood Scrubs.
65. French Fields.

TEST 6

1. Angela Douglas.
2. The screams of a dying soldier.
3. 'I'm not going to sit here like a spare lemon, waiting for the squeezer.'
4. On board an aeroplane.
5. Dr Henderson.
6. Thunderbolt.
7. Barbados.
8. Eight million.
9. London.
10. Sir Keith Gold.
11. The Skye Boat Song.
12. The dematerialisation circuit.
13. North Wales.
14. A Time Sensor – described by Jo as a 'TARDIS sniffer-outer'.
15. HMS *Aphrodite*.
16. Sacrifice.
17. By exploding a star and creating a black hole.

18. *The Time Warrior*.
19. Whether or not she is free of the Mara's influence.
20. A dinosaur.
21. Professor Herbert Clegg.
22. Think Tank.
23. By including a line of dialogue: 'There's a report in from the Met Office, Sir. There are freak weather conditions over the whole area.'
24. St Paul's Cathedral.
25. Peter Halliday.
26. The Duke of Forgill.
27. The Main Research Reactor building.
28. A Raston Warrior Robot.
29. An apple.
30. Lake Vortigren.
31. Brazil.
32. Professor Stahlman. *Inferno*.
33. Jo Grant. *Terror of the Autons*.
34. The TARDIS lock has a metabolism detector.
35. Tommy Godber.
36. The human eye.
37. Mawdryn.
38. Irongron. *The Time Warrior*.
39. A machine in an old leather satchel.
40. *The Three Doctors*.
41. Professor Kettlewell's brain pattern, the robot's inventor.
42. Matha Jones (Freema Agyeman). She had to

pull out when signed to appear in Law & Order UK.

43. A Time Disturbance Sensor.
44. Senator Alcott.
45. They set fire to it.
46. Callandra.
47. Treasure.
48. Bessie.
49. Marshal J Grover.
50. Louis Marks.
51. A Yeti. By igniting a firework, a Galactic Glitter.
52. Nerve toxins.
53. Krasis.
54. The publishers (Target) wanted the character left alive for a possible sequel.
55. M3 Variant.
56. Salutua.
57. Cave paintings.
58. Loch Ness.
59. The Destroyer. *Battlefield*.
60. A Doberman. Stahlman's Ooze (*Inferno*).
61. The World Peace Conference (as detailed in the TV story *The Mind of Evil*).
62. By paddling across in an old coal truck.
63. Hull.
64. The Time Lords.
65. Sadie Miller, daughter of Elisabeth Sladen.

TEST 7

1. Miss Hawthorne. Damaris Hayman.
2. The Cyber Planner.
3. 'Lethbridge-Stewart. My dear fellow. How nice to see you again'.
4. Bentley T Series.
5. The Lamadeens.
6. Daleks; Cybermen; Ice Warriors; Silurians; War Machines; Zarbi; Koquillian.
7. The village of Aldbury.
8. Sergeant Osgood.
9. Black.
10. A tin foil hat.
11. 23.
12. 'You'd never believe me'.
13. Carey Blyton.
14. HAVOC
15. Greg Sutton. Kuwait.
16. 'More like the Queen Mary than a spaceship'.
17. A packet of tea laced with a phosphorescent fungus that makes him feel ill.

18. Russia.
19. He 'faded away, like a ghost' right in front of Sergeant Benton's eyes.
20. The Rose and Crown.
21. The window cleaner falls from his ladder in 'slow motion'.
22. He was a regular character in 'Emmerdale Farm' at the time and the producers would not release him.
23. Sergeant Benton.
24. The monthly inspection.
25. Nuton Power Complex.
26. Half a dozen leading scientists and several million pounds worth of ultra secret equipment.
27. To revive them from hibernation.
28. Brook Cottage.
29. Mortimer.
30. That he's a 'swinger'.
31. *The Web of Fear* (spoken by The Intelligence).
32. The Brigadier's kilt.
33. Anthony Ainley.
34. Professor Travers in *The Web of Fear*.
35. Lomax.
36. 3 weeks.
37. He got lost in the time vortex. The TARDIS brought him home.
38. Peter Warmsly.
39. polly@worldwide.com.
40. The Judgementors.

41. The British Museum.

42. The inside of the TARDIS.

43. Romana and Leela. They travel to the Dark Tower in the Death Zone.

44. *The Midwich Cuckoos.*

45. Tegan.

46. The Doctor.

47. Old Jones the Milk.

48. Dynastrene.

49. Kebiria.

50. Marmalade.

51. 'Like trying to fly a second hand gas stove.'

52. *Colony in Space.*

53. *The One Second Hour.*

54. The Ambush!

55. 'Chauvinist.'

56. He shoots the Demon with silver bullets loaded in his service revolver.

57. Time travellers from the future.

58. A device the Doctor calls the 'door handle'.

59. Doctor Omega.

60. 200 years.

61. Professor Eric Stahlman (*Inferno*).

62. Rembrandt.

63. Because it is a Mark 2 circuit. The Doctor's TARDIS uses a Mark 1 circuit.

64. Radioactive isotope.

65. *Shelley, Yes, Prime Minister, Sink or Swim, Only Fools and Horses*

TEST 8

1. *Liberty Hall* (2009).
2. 'So, now I've hung up my uniform for good... unless I hear that a blue police box has been found somewhere, and then, don't you worry, I'll be ready!'
3. Sticky tape on the windows.
4. On a motorbike.
5. Henlow Down.
6. Robert Holmes.
7. Dracula's Castle.
8. Samson's car – a Lotus Super Seven.
9. Trans-migration of object.
10. They always keep a well stocked larder, not to mention the cellar (wine).
11. 'Wouldn't advise you to try.'
12. Sevilla.
13. The Save Planet Earth Society. 'Last Chance for Man.'
14. Professor Stahlman.

15. Daffodils.
16. Donald Hewlett.
17. The credentials of the real Adjudicator.
18. 20 miles.
19. A metamorphic symbiosis regenerator.
20. 'Really.'
21. The Cyclotron.
22. Uxarieus.
23. Sector 27.
24. Packer.
25. Jupiter. Venus.
26. His hair brushes a cobweb with a large spider resident in it.
27. Karate chops a brick in half.
28. Angus Ferguson McRanald.
29. Evans.
30. Timothy Combe.
31. Beacon Hill Research Establishment (Ministry of Technology).
32. Ministry of Technology.
33. The Star Warrior.
34. *The Daemons.*
35. Stonehenge.
36. Dr Petra Williams.
37. The Time Lords.
38. Warrant Officer.
39. Mike Yates. Liz Shaw.
40. Mike Yates.
41. Santa Claus.

42. 3000 years.
43. Huxley.
44. A game of football.
45. In the stag's head.
46. 'It has a graveyard stench.'
47. A damaged alien computer.
48. 'That's a fearsome looking load of electronic nonsense you've got together, Dr Ingram.'
49. United Galactic Intelligence Taskforce.
50. Lhasa.
51. By using their Mind Analysis Machine.
52. James Stevens. Daily Chronicle.
53. Because his pension has been cancelled.
54. 'Mushrooming?'
55. *The Magic Box.*
56. 'Are you any good with the lawnmower, Ancelyn?'
57. Borusa.
58. They were all defeated by the man known as The Doctor.
59. A Time Flow Analogue.
60. Tea Leaves.
61. Ogmore-by-Sea.
62. WOTAN (The War Machines).
63. Mr Hibbert.
64. A Jelly Baby.
65. Tim Gambrell.

TEST 9

1. 'What is three times seven, times four, minus thirty-five?'
2. Helen Worth.
3. 30 seconds.
4. 'Oh Well'. Fleetwood Mac.
5. HM Prison Strangmoor.
6. The Doctor salutes the Brigadier, who is in Cyberman Avatar form and has just vaporised Missy (The Master).
7. Dr Strangelove.
8. Murder. For blowing up the Silurians' base.
9. Daughter of Light.
10. Private Upton.
11. *Inferno*.
12. The first night of bombing, during the Blitz.
13. 'A most good humoured wine. A touch sardonic perhaps, but not cynical. A most civilised wine, one after my own heart.'
14. 'Just can't dematerialise.'

15. By remotely releasing sleeping gas into the console room.
16. Jimmy.
17. His right side.
18. The Brigadier's white open top Mercedes sports car (Reg. No. BLC 7B).
19. Finland.
20. Ian Gilmore.
21. 'The brakes work by the absorption of inertia, including yours.'
22. It is able to teleport itself.
23. Minsbridge Wildlife Sanctuary.
24. Arthur Ollis.
25. He lulls him into a false sense of security by enquiring whether he is being looked after okay and if he has had a cup of tea, before yelling at him, 'Stand to attention when you're talking to me and call me Sir.' The captive immediately stands to attention and shouts, 'Sir!'
26. A pretty yellow flower.
27. *Robot*.
28. Explosives 808.
29. An apple.
30. 3.
31. Shada.
32. Under his hat. Liz Shaw's pass.
33. Mr Brownrose.
34. They are all 'government types'. There are no

famous personalities.

35. His wife, Margaret.
36. A stun gun.
37. On the head of a suit of armour.
38. The Beatles.
39. Liz Shaw.
40. Because it would be the end of the Doctor as a Time Lord.
41. A rain machine.
42. The Nightmare.
43. K'anpo.
44. 'Smash Hit'.
45. As 'living metal with the capacity to grow like a living organism'.
46. Aylesbury Grange, UNIT's special detention centre.
47. As a heartbeat.
48. A suspended animation machine.
49. Light green.
50. French.
51. Mrs Griffiths.
52. UFO sightings and supernatural occurrences.
53. 1822.
54. The Master.
55. On a 'video wrist watch'.
56. Zoe and Jamie.
57. The unnatural wind causes the signpost to rotate.
58. Tell a story; make a thing; sing a song.

59. A motor tricycle.
60. Orange.
61. Dr Tyler.
62. H37 Compound.
63. Jamie.
64. Darren Carlin.
65. Cambridge.

TEST 10

1. Doctor Runciman.
2. The television and a plate of corned beef sandwiches.
3. International Mining Company.
4. America.
5. Professor Kettering.
6. Blimey; Danger Patrol; Invisible Woman X; Les Granby's Laugh-a-Long.
7. General Finch.
8. *The Eight Doctors* by Terrence Dicks.
9. The Cloven Hoof.
10. The Doctor. Jo is being held hostage in the Master's TARDIS.
11. A helicopter dropping smoke bombs.
12. To power a trial run of the TARDIS console.
13. The Master.
14. The Nestene Consciousness.
15. Sergeant Benton. A bite to eat.
16. Room For Living.

17. Stravinsky.
18. Euston Square.
19. A tractor.
20. The Doctor ties Sullivan up and hangs him in a cupboard.
21. Major Branwell.
22. The Eye of Orion.
23. Chronos.
24. Lavinia Smith. A virologist.
25. Waverley Oil Field.
26. Planting a rosebush in his garden.
27. 29,000 light years.
28. Major Baker.
29. A spaceship.
30. *The Hollow Man of Carrington Lodge.*
31. Robert Louis Stevenson.
32. *The Claws of Axos.*
33. A telephone engineer.
34. Bermondsey.
35. To find out how it works. The Doctor wants to revive the Silurians one at a time as they have a wealth of scientific knowledge.
36. With his sonic screwdriver.
37. Melvyn Hayes.
38. Mike Yates.
39. Glittering purple shells.
40. St Pancras.
41. To detonate the mines in the minefield.
42. Skang.

43. Tina Packer.
44. Windmill 347.
45. The 'Whomobile'.
46. A monastery.
47. Corporal Palmer.
48. Fennel; sesame (the recipe the Doctor concocts as a sleep draught to incapacitate Irongron and his men).
49. Oregon.
50. By summoning a knight on horseback armed with a lance to charge at the vehicles.
51. A group of 17th century Roundheads.
52. 'Like a cross between Guy Fawkes and Halloween.'
53. The London Underground.
54. To reverse all the systems.
55. An oil shaft in Arabia.
56. Sonic screwdriver.
57. 'Keep in the shadows. We've some disagreeable fellow passengers.'
58. The Brigadier is distracted by questions about UNIT funding and 'problems at home'.
59. A high impulse blanket frequency.
60. Rachel.
61. The Dalek voices.
62. Dunstanton Lake.
63. *The Ark in Space. The Sontaran Experiment.*
64. John Smith, Dr John Smith.
65. Two of everything.

TEST 11

1. Driver Evans.
2. *The Life of Evans*. John Peel.
3. The Crab Nebula.
4. Because it is invisible having landed in the middle of a field.
5. The Warkeeper's Crown.
6. A tattoo.
7. 'Kilroy Was Here.'
8. Switzerland. 112.
9. They were under the impression that a real church had been blown up, when in fact it was a model.
10. Mailer.
11. Johnny Kidd & The Pirates.
12. Temporal displacement.
13. Several pages have been torn out.
14. 'He left the army in 1979. Sells second had cars somewhere.'
15. John Wakefield.

16. 2471.
17. He blocks the road with Bessie, asks the hijackers to help him push the car out of the way and then arms Bessie's 'Anti Theft Device' which adheres the hijackers to the car's bodywork.
18. No. 2 Output Pipe.
19. Corporal Nutting.
20. Rank has its privileges. 'Empress of Mars'.
21. NCB (National Coal Board), Cardiff.
22. Flip Collins.
23. Through the window.
24. She thinks the missing Professor Rubeish might be hiding in there.
25. Professor Clifford Jones.
26. Dr Ruth Ingram. Stuart Hyde.
27. The Brigadier's wristwatch.
28. The Doctor's long scarf.
29. A chicken leg.
30. Heat from the Bunsen burner.
31. Sister Lamont.
32. As a touch of cosmic angst.
33. The Gore Crown Hotel.
34. Snow Bear.
35. In a broom cupboard in a London Underground station.
36. By playing a tune on a harp. The notes for the tune are shown in the portrait of a Time Lord playing a harp on the wall panel which opens

to reveal the Time Scoop control room.

37. Birmingham.
38. A stimulant.
39. It kills her.
40. A tank.
41. Culverton.
42. The quest for the Key to Time.
43. 'If I reverse the polarity of the neutron flow...'
44. The Yeti.
45. The right hand one.
46. The blue sapphire crystal from Metebelis 3.
47. He becomes hypnotised by the crystal himself.
48. 'Control.'
49. Bill McLaren.
50. Jenny Winterleaf.
51. Most are ex-SAS professionals.
52. The First Doctor.
53. The Doctor, Jo Grant, Mike Yates.
54. It is pulled from a ditch by a farmer and his tractor.
55. Artificial scenarios in which the Doctor sacrifices his life to save Jo, the Brigadier, Susan, Zoe and others.
56. RAF Manston.
57. Sergeant Benton.
58. As the chameleon of the elements, a thinking molecule.
59. 'Well, here we go again.'
60. Behind the book shelves in the castle's library.

61. A car to replace the one he 'stole' from the hospital.
62. Ruby Slant.
63. A city gent complete with bowler hat and umbrella.
64. Peter Bryant.
65. Monks (they are referred to as friars by Irongron's castle guards).

TEST 12

1. PC Groom.
2. Delphon.
3. Captain Yates.
4. Stormwatch.
5. Private Ogden.
6. A test tube full of red fluid.
7. What is the capital of Australia? How many beans make five?
8. Unity Is Strength.
9. 'Always remember, an army marches on its stomach.'
10. The Earth Adjudicator.
11. The Second Doctor's recorder.
12. Major General Rutlidge.
13. Bert Pritchard. Dai Evans.
14. One million.
15. A flattened dandelion flower.
16. *The Scales of Injustice* (Missing Adventures series) by Gary Russell.

17. Geoffrey Burgon.
18. A frog.
19. The Fertility Dance.
20. Arthur's Ale.
21. Yeti (from *The Web of Fear*).
22. Colonel Creighton.
23. An extra glass of brandy in case the Doctor came to visit.
24. Space 1999.
25. Douglas Camfield.
26. Alistair and James's service numbers on a telephone keypad.
27. The Pengriffen Arms.
28. Mars Probe 7.
29. Don Harper.
30. *The Edge of Destruction* (First Doctor story, 1964).
31. Eagle.
32. Mike Yates.
33. Drashigs.
34. Like a disappointed bloodhound.
35. 'The Gang's Back Again'. Kool And The Gang.
36. Dr Meredith.
37. It involves a lot of chasing and running.
38. John-Paul and Ringo-George.
39. Tayborough Sands.
40. Geneva.
41. A stand up comedian.

42. Alex Macintosh.
43. Leicestershire.
44. The Master.
45. Peter Moffatt.
46. A 'crop circle' (actually a series of square-sided shapes) that are filled with ice.
47. The Seventh Doctor.
48. By disguising himself as a provisions delivery van driver.
49. Ian Chesterton and Barbara Wright.
50. Barry Letts.
51. Upside down.
52. Alec Whistler.
53. Robert Soloman.
54. Michael Alexander Raymond Yates.
55. Hal.
56. Shrunk down and in a sandwich box.
57. Tadcaster.
58. The Soviets.
59. As a computer cabinet.
60. 'Signal S.O.S.'.
61. It is wearing a real wristwatch, wound up and adjusted to the correct time.
62. The Hebrides.
63. Make a full inventory of the HQ.
64. The future.
65. On a disused army firing range.

Available from Candy Jar Books

THE LUCY WILSON MYSTERIES: AVATARS OF THE INTELLIGENCE
by Sue Hampton

Lucy Wilson doesn't want to move from London to sleepy South Wales. But when she arrives at her new seaside home, it doesn't appear to be as boring as she expected.

Ogmore-by-Sea seems to be under the control of a mysterious and powerful force. But why is Lucy its target? And why, when students at her new school start to disappear, does no one seem to care?

With the help of her new friend Hobo, Lucy Wilson must assume the mantle of her grandfather, the legendary Brigadier Lethbridge-Stewart, and defeat an invisible enemy before it's too late.

ISBN: 978-0-9957436-9-4

Also available from Candy Jar Books

LETHBRIDGE-STEWART: NIGHT OF THE INTELLIGENCE
by Andy Frankham-Allen

Three men feel the pull of the Great Intelligence.

One; Professor Edward Travers, who was once possessed by it, plans to return to the Det-Sen Monastery to clear his mind of the Intelligence once and for all. But he never makes it. The Vault want him, but an old friend is waiting in the wings to help.

Two; Owain Vine, who carries the seed of the Intelligence within, is in Japan on a pilgrimage to cleanse himself of the taint he feels in his soul. Soon a happy reunion takes place, and Owain learns that past friendships are not what they seemed.

Three; Brigadier Alistair Lethbridge-Stewart, who finds himself haunted by the spectre of his brother, James, who refuses to stay dead.

The stage is set for the long, dark night of the Intelligence.

ISBN: 978-0-9957436-3-2

Also available from Candy Jar Books

LETHBRIDGE-STEWART: THE DREAMER'S LAMENT
by Benjamin-Burford Jones

While visiting his mother, Lethbridge-Stewart is a little perturbed when Harold Chorley calls to ask for his help. A train from Bristol has gone missing, and Chorley is convinced it has something to do with the Keynsham Triangle, where over fifty people have vanished without trace since the early 1800s.

Elsewhere, Anne Travers is coming to terms with a loss in her family, and sets about preparing for a funeral. However, news reaches her that both Lethbridge-Stewart and Chorley have gone missing, and her help is required to find them. And, hopefully, solve the mystery of the Keynsham Triangle.

What connects the missing train to the Triangle, what has it got to do with a Wren from the 1940s, and just why does it appear that Lethbridge-Stewart and Chorley are in the village of Keynsham in 1815?

ISBN: 978-0-9957436-5-6